Dogmania

Other Books by Allan Zullo
and Mara Bovsun

Amazing but True Bird Tales
Mews Items
Amazing but True Fishing Tales

Dogmania

AMAZING BUT TRUE
CANINE STORIES

by
Allan Zullo
and
Mara Bovsun

**Andrews McMeel
Publishing**

Kansas City

06 07 08 09 10 BID 10 9 8 7 6 5 4 3 2 1

ISBN-13: 978-0-7407-5772-3
ISBN-10: 0-7407-5772-5

Library of Congress Control Number: 2005933901

Design by Pete Lippincott

www.andrewsmcmeel.com

ATTENTION: SCHOOLS AND BUSINESSES

Andrews McMeel books are available at quantity discounts with bulk purchase for educational, business, or sales promotional use. For information, please write to: Special Sales Department, Andrews McMeel Publishing, LLC, 4520 Main Street, Kansas City, Missouri 64111.

To the Bensons—Ray, Jodi, McKinley,
and Delaney—and to the Hamanns—
Zeke, Jill, Maureen, and Margaret— for being
such warm, fun, and loving people.

—A.Z.

To Coppy, who waited every day
at the El for my father to come home from
World War II, and to Maggie and Lisa,
who never cease to amaze me.

—M.B.

Contents

Acknowledgments

W E ARE EXTREMELY GRATEFUL to all the dog owners, dog lovers, and veterinarians who graciously shared their remarkable stories with us.

In addition we wish to thank the following: Debra Nier; Animal Haven Shelter, New York City (www.animalhavenshelter.org); the Burlington County Animal Alliance (www.bcaaofnj.org); the Mayor's Alliance for New York City's Animals (www.animalalliancenyc.org); Hearing Dogs for Deaf People (www.hearing-dogs.co.uk); Laura James of Leonberger Rescue, Inc. (www.leonberger-rescue.org); and Little Shelter Animal Rescue (www.littleshelter.com); and Petfinder.com

Do you have a dog story you would like to share? Do you want to see what other books the authors have written? Go to www.allanzullo.com.

Top Dogs

N O DOMESTICATED ANIMAL is more bonded to humans than the dog. More than 60 million canines in the United States have burrowed their way into our hearts. They guard homes, pull sleds, fetch sticks, herd livestock, protect kids, catch crooks, serve the disabled, and sniff out contraband. That is, of course, when they aren't making us laugh at their antics and escapades or making us teary-eyed with their devotion and loyalty. They might be eager to play but they are even more eager to please. And they ask for little more than a pat on the head and a biscuit in their mouth.

This book is a celebration of remarkable canines whose actions and adventures have astounded and amused their owners and admirers. In the following pages, you'll read a collection of amazing but true stories about:

- Unforgettable dogs such as Jasper the black Lab mix who checked himself into a hospital after he was struck by a car . . . Samson the German shepherd mix who acts as a guide dog for his blind canine sweetheart Delilah . . . and Faith the service dog who, when her disabled owner passed out, called 911, barked in the phone, and then unlocked the door for police.

- Canine survivors who cheated death, like Sport the beagle who was struck by lightning . . . Cooper the golden retriever who was attacked by a monster alligator . . . and Sweetie the terrier who emerged from her grave after she was mistakenly buried alive.

- Wacky dogs who wound up in trouble, such as Rancher the blue heeler who locked his owner out of a pickup truck, put it in gear, and drove the vehicle into a tree . . . Tasha the Jack Russell terrier who dug a tunnel from his owner's basement into a neighbor's home . . . and Liza the yellow Lab who swallowed a wedding ring the day before her owners' marriage ceremony.

- Courageous dogs like Buster the springer spaniel who uncovered a cache of weapons and explosives hidden by an armed resistance cell in southern Iraq . . . Casper the little shih tzu who helped her owner fend off a would-be rapist and then provided DNA evidence that convicted him . . . and Rocky the Rhodesian ridgeback who prevented an intruder from kidnapping a little girl.

Whether purebreds or mongrels, show dogs or lapdogs, one thing is certain: Dogs have been our most loyal four-legged animals since the beginning of civilization . . . and they'll remain by our sides for as long as we love them.

Scamps

T'WAS A WEEK BEFORE CHRISTMAS and all through the house, not a creature was stirring—except for a rambunctious puppy named Athos.

And, oh, what holiday memories he made for his owners, Michele and David Cohen in 2000. They lived in a rural area in upstate New York with their four large lionlike dogs called Leonbergers—Gypsy, Java, and Angus and his son Athos, a nine-month-old, 120-pound bundle of trouble.

Athos was always getting into some kind of mischief. Any item left on a table was fair game to steal. The puppy would grab the object, charge out the doggy door—built jumbo-size (three feet by two feet) to accommodate these huge

lionesque dogs—and bury it in the backyard,
usually after he had chewed it beyond recognition.

Nevertheless, it still came as a shock to the
Cohens when, during the puppy's first holiday
season, Athos turned into the canine version
of the grinch who stole Christmas.

Michele wanted to make this holiday the one
she had dreamed of her whole life. No expense
was spared in choosing the ornaments for the
Christmas tree. They were beautiful—gold,
silver, and sparkling glass, some handmade,
others expensive Lenox china in the shape of
snowflakes, angels, and stars.

Michele spent hours hanging ornaments on
the seven-foot-tall Norway spruce and decorating
the house with red silk poinsettias and bunting.
On the living room coffee table, she displayed
a three-foot-tall centerpiece made of gold
pinecones in the shape of a Christmas tree.

Athos sat by quietly, keeping his eye on her
as one by one, she placed little figurines on the
branches. He especially liked the ones that had
bells on them.

By about 11 p.m. all the decorations were just the way Michele had wanted them. Everything looked perfect. After turning on holiday music, she and David had some wine and admired the beautiful living room. "I felt like Donna Reed," she recalled in a personal interview. Then the couple and their four pets walked up the festively decorated stairs to the bedroom and fell into a sound slumber.

Or at least all did except Athos.

When Michele opened her eyes the next morning, she gazed out the window and saw a beautiful layer of fresh snow blanketing her property. It was a gorgeous morning that left her feeling warm and fuzzy.

But when she sat up and looked over at the floor where her dogs were sleeping, she could only shake her head in amusement. The three adult dogs were covered in toilet paper. Sometime during the night, Athos had grabbed a roll of toilet paper out of the bathroom, brought it into the bedroom, and draped the tissue all over the dogs. "They looked like mummies," she said.

If only that were all that Athos had done during the night.

After removing the "tissue nightshirts," Michele glanced outside and realized that her young canine delinquent had more holiday surprises in store. Gold pinecones—the remains of her three-foot high centerpiece—were scattered across the deck.

"Then I saw the Christmas tree—the entire tree," she recalled. "It was outside."

Somehow Athos had knocked over the seven-foot tree, picked it up, and carried it across the room. Then he managed to yank it through the large doggy door and drag it into the yard. Broken, crushed, and chewed ornaments littered the deck and the snow-covered ground. Michele said, "He was standing behind the tree with a happy expression on his face, as if to say, 'See how much better it looks out here?'"

As the Cohens surveyed the wreckage, Athos' father Angus wandered toward the back of the fence where the snow was covered in what looked like blood. On closer inspection, the

Cohens were somewhat relieved to see that none of the animals had been bleeding. The red was just more of Michele's Christmas cheer. "My silk poinsettias, gone to the dogs," she lamented.

Oddly, other than some broken ornaments and glass shards, there were few signs that the Christmas tree had been lugged through the house. Michele figured that after Athos knocked the tree down, he grabbed it in the middle, lifted it, and gingerly carried it to the doggy door and dropped it. Then he went through and, from there, tugged on the tree until it was outside. The couple had been so tired from decorating all day that they had slept through Athos' tree-napping.

The ghosts of Christmas trashed lasted well into spring for the Cohens because chewed-up ornaments kept surfacing from under the thawing snow. Michele never again put up a big Christmas tree.

TASHA THE JACK RUSSELL TERRIER loved to dig holes—deep and long ones. In fact, she once dug a tunnel from the basement of her owner's house to his neighbor's.

The dog was owned by Philip Salmon who, in the 1990s, lived in one of many attached Victorian row houses in the Beaconsfield section of Toronto, Canada. The houses, built in the late 1800s, were simple yet stylish two-story, two-bedroom homes with packed-earth basement floors.

Tasha's favorite pastime was digging, and the basement was her playground. She had learned to open the antique latch to the basement door that led down the few worn, wooden steps to the dirt floor. Then she would dig to her heart's content. "We often came home from shopping to find her peeking through the open basement door, her face covered in dust and soil," Salmon wrote in badpets.net.

One day he was visiting his next-door neighbors and left Tasha home alone. Through the wall that separated the two houses, Tasha heard lots of laughing, and wanted to be a part of the fun. So she went down into the basement and started digging. But this time, it wasn't just a hole in the floor. She burrowed a tunnel under the wall dividing the two homes.

"Somehow she knew where to dig this tunnel because she found a break in the rubble footing, came up on the other side of the dividing wall, and started barking at the neighbors' basement door," Salmon said.

At first they thought the barks were coming from Salmon's home. "We commented on how loud it was and that we hadn't realized how sound really traveled from one house to the next," he said.

"Tasha grew impatient and started scratching at the door. It was at this point we realized that somehow she had become locked in our neighbors' basement. When we opened the door, we were greeted by a very pink tongue sticking out from a very dirty face that was attached to a dirt-covered body. Her normally white hair was now charcoal gray and the face was as black as coal. On investigation, we came to realize what she had done. She had escaped the loneliness of her own home and found the party going on next door."

A CROOKED CANINE was collared by police after he was caught on a surveillance camera stealing an elderly woman's garden statues.

According to police, in April 2004, Ruth Breiner, seventy-five, of McLean, Virginia, noticed that a ceramic baby raccoon was stolen from a set of small animal figurines in her yard. The thief returned June 7 and made off with a fawn. A replacement deer disappeared June 14, and a squirrel two days later.

Breiner suspected she was the target of a not-so-funny prank, so she contacted Fairfax County Police. Officers installed a surveillance camera in Breiner's bedroom window, and it wasn't long before they knew who the perp was—a black Labrador retriever.

On three different occasions, the camera caught the felonious pooch enter Breiner's yard late at night, scout his surroundings for eyewitnesses, and then make off with a garden statue in his mouth. The dog was seen on tape filching a squirrel, a chipmunk, and a fox. But neither Breiner nor the police knew where the dog lived, so in July police released the video to the local media in hopes of identifying the suspect. The footage received wide play, including national coverage.

On July 9, the embarrassed owners, who asked that their names not be used, came forward with their dog Magnum. The couple went to Breiner's house and began apologizing profusely before handing over the ceramic fawns, chipmunk, squirrel, and fox that their dog had swiped in the dead of night. The 110-pound canine bandit just sat on Breiner's stoop while the forgiving woman patted his head.

"He was just sitting there, that silly dog," Breiner told the *Washington Post*. "I couldn't get mad at him. They are big, old, slobbering dogs that are friendly as all that."

Officer Sophia Grinan told reporters that Magnum's owners learned of their dog's kleptomania after a friend saw footage of the Lab's misdemeanors on a local station's news report and told the couple about it. The owners became suspicious and soon found Magnum's stash of ceramic animals hidden in their backyard.

Magnum wasn't sent to the pen for his crimes. "Dogs don't have criminal intent and cannot be prosecuted," Grinan said. "To this date we don't make handcuffs for dogs." However, the owners promised to keep him under closer scrutiny.

Police said they didn't know Magnum's motive, but Breiner, who was happy to have her animals back home, noted that the dog is a retriever. She said the detective who viewed the surveillance tape told her Magnum never sniffed

the statues first; he just picked them up and
ran off.

Breiner said she was thankful for one thing:
"The dog never bothered the baby rabbits or the
mama rabbit, and they were the most expensive
of all."

A BLUE HEELER NAMED RANCHER wound up in
the doghouse after he locked his owner out of
a pickup truck, put it in gear, and drove the
vehicle into a tree.

On his 1,200-acre farm near Alva, Oklahoma,
Lyle Sneary, sixty-seven, had his dog with him as
he checked on his cattle in a pasture after a
snowfall in February 2002. Sneary stopped the
1993 Dodge pickup truck after he spotted a
downed cow that had recently given birth.

In a personal interview, Sneary said, "I got
out to tend to the cow, but I left Rancher inside.
I had turned off the engine, put it in park, and
rolled the window down about four inches. I was

about twelve feet from the truck and giving the cow some feed. Some cows saw this and figured that maybe she was getting something better than they were, so they wandered over toward the front of the pickup.

"When they got close, I hollered at them to get away. Well, when he heard me holler, he thought that meant he needed to come unglued inside the cab. He jumped up against the door on the driver's side and hit the automatic button that locked it. But I didn't know it at the time.

"Then he kept barking and leaped on the dashboard and knocked the gearshift lever out of park and into neutral. The pickup was parked on the downward slope of a little hill. When I saw the pickup rolling downhill, I chased after it and jumped on the running board.

"I tried to open the door but it was locked. Then I stuck my arm in the opening in the window trying to unlock the door so I could get to the steering wheel, but I just couldn't quite reach the lock. The pickup was gathering more speed. For some reason, the vehicle made a little bit of a left turn and headed right for a tree. Whether Rancher turned the steering wheel, I can't say because I was so busy. All I know is he was sitting in the front seat watching all of this.

"The tree was coming up real fast, so I bailed out and the pickup rammed into that tree real hard—hard enough where the insurance company declared it a total loss."

Fortunately, Rancher was not hurt. Unfortunately, his owner was angry at him. "I was so doggone mad at him that I wouldn't let him out of the pickup," he said. Sneary had to trudge a mile and a half in the deep snow in freezing temperatures to a shed where he had left his cell phone. When he reached the shed, he called his wife to come and get him.

Eventually Sneary forgave his blue heeler. "Rancher is a good dog, just like his daddy, Farmer, was," he said. "Every time I go out to check the cows, Rancher goes with me. And for safety reasons, I let him ride up front rather than in the back of the pickup. He's saved me a thousand miles of walking when I've got cows out.

"And he's saved my hide many times when I come into town after dark because in my area there are a zillion deer and about every week someone runs into a deer and smashes up their vehicle. That dog stands attentive and even when it's dark he'll alert me that there's something out there and I slow down. He sees what I don't see."

When word of Rancher's escapade spread, Sneary took a ribbing from friends, including Oklahoma Highway Patrol Trooper Chris West. Sneary recalled, "He called me and said, 'I'm going to have to revoke Rancher's driver's license.'"

No dog caused more trouble for an army officer than Riley the fox terrier. He almost got his master kicked out of the service.

Riley was a spoiled four-legged hellion. He was also the constant companion of Lt. Col. Clarence Deems, commanding officer of the

U.S. Army's Fort Howard in Baltimore. A widower, the colonel focused all his affection on his pet dog, allowing the canine full run of the army post, much to the dismay of the other officers and enlisted men who were often the target of the terrier's bad behavior.

The dog caused such havoc on the post that finally several officers brought charges of incompetence against Lt. Col. Deems and tried to get him removed from duty in 1908. The colonel was forced to appear at a War Department hearing to defend himself and his canine companion.

Among the charges leveled against Lt. Col. Deems was his total lack of discipline of his dog, because Riley:

- Would crazily run around the parade ground during marching drills, right through the ranks, barking at the officers and snapping at their heels

- Would eat at the mess hall table with the other officers

- Left nasty fleas on the bus that carried officers' wives into town

- Stole one of his master's boots and hid it, forcing the post commander to hobble around for an hour with one foot bootless

- Would lick Deems on the lips while officers were forced to stand at attention

- Would chase certain officers and enlisted men through the barracks

When it was Lt. Col. Deems's turn to testify, he didn't deny any of the charges. However, he went out of his way to praise his canine comrade. "I live all alone, and the dog is a great comfort to me, and I see no reason to be ashamed of it," he said. "I must admit also that he thinks a great deal of me and sometimes jumps all over me. As for being fed at the table, the little fellow has been trained to stand up on his hind legs and beg for a bit of food and sometimes I do throw him a morsel." He added that at times when Riley ran through the ranks, "I tried to call him back, but he wouldn't come."

When the hearing ended, the army ruled that although Riley was definitely a feisty and mischievous dog, he had done nothing seriously wrong—and neither had his master. In fact, two months later, Deems was promoted to full colonel and given a new army post, Fort Hancock. No one was more pleased about the move than the officers at Fort Howard who would no longer be harassed by Riley.

A DOG HELPED CONVINCE A JUDGE to free his master from jail.

William G. Reising went everywhere with his wire-haired Irish terrier, Blucher—his day job as a laborer in New York City, his poker games at night, and his friends' homes where, it seemed, they were always partying.

On Labor Day, 1904, Reising partied a little bit too much and became rowdy outside an apartment building. When Officer Nick Griffith told him to move on, Reising protested. One word led to another and he was arrested.

When Griffith started leading Reising away, Blucher tugged at the officer's pant leg and wouldn't let go. Reising then made a deal with the policeman: In exchange for calling off his dog, Reising was allowed to have Blucher accompany him to the police station and stay with him in the holding cell until he faced the judge.

The next day, with his dog by his side, Reising appeared in the Jefferson Market Court. After hearing Griffith's testimony, Magistrate Mayo fined Reising $3. Reising was unable to pay the fine so he was sentenced to three days in jail. Upon hearing the ruling, Blucher barked angrily at the judge.

The dog followed Reising as he was led away by Griffith. But when the jail keeper saw Blucher, he wouldn't let the dog stay in the cell with his master, raising a howl of protest from Reising. The jail keeper then told Griffith to take charge of the dog, but the officer refused.

Unable to resolve their differences, the three—along with Blucher—went back to the judge and explained the situation. Magistrate Mayo laughed and then decided to free Reising and cancel the fine.

The *New York Times* said, "If ever a small Irish terrier looked triumphant, Blucher did as his master carried him out of the courtroom clasped in his arms."

A DOG SAVED HIMSELF and his master from serious trouble with the law when he "testified" in court that he was not mean.

The New Jersey Department of Health had charged Africa, a six-year-old dalmatian, with being a vicious dog. His owner, Mary Salari, of Newark, had also been charged with allowing a vicious dog to roam free in the neighborhood where it was alleged Africa had bitten three people. The health department wanted to lock up Africa and fine his master.

On March 3, 1950, Mrs. Salari and Africa showed up in court to defend themselves against the charges. The owner admitted that her dog often wandered around the neighborhood, but claimed that the dalmatian was a sweet dog who would never hurt anyone. To back up her claim, she presented a statement signed by thirty-one neighbors who said Africa was not vicious.

Then it was Africa's turn to defend himself. He trotted up to the bench, and without any prompting from his owner, wagged his tail and offered his paw to the judge. When the judge shook the dog's paw, Africa licked the judge's hand.

Moments later, the judge made his ruling: Africa should not be locked up and Mrs. Salari should not be fined. The court, however, ordered that Africa had to be on a leash whenever he left home.

THE VERY DOG who was supposed to guard a factory from theft turned out to be a serial thief who was stealing the company's expensive rolls of copper wire.

The factory, FLZ in Bor, Yugoslavia, had been the target of a cunning thief who was filching valuable rolls of copper from the storeroom in the fall of 2002. Authorities were baffled because there were no signs of any forced entry, security personnel never detected any intruders, and workers were searched. Besides, Jackie the guard dog hadn't given any alerts or warning barks.

The factory was losing hundreds of dollars in pilfered copper balls each night, so management decided to install a security camera in an effort to nail the culprit. Days later, they discovered it was an inside job because the camera clearly showed the identity of the miscreant. It was Jackie.

She had been sneaking into the storeroom through a small hole in the wall to swipe the copper rolls. She took them out into the factory yard and buried them.

A factory spokesperson told the Yugoslav newspaper *Glas Javnosti*, "While the men were watching the perimeter, the dog was behind them stealing the merchandise—and covering her tracks by burying her loot.

"There seems to be something about the smell of the wire, which is treated with a special protective coat, that the dog liked, and she was burying them, presumably for a rainy day. Dogs will often bury food that is too hard to eat because it softens in the ground."

With the help of a metal detector, factory personnel were able to recover most of Jackie's buried loot.

Employers decided not to prosecute, and she was allowed to remain on the job—as long as the storeroom was kept "dog proof."

AT THE HOME OF HIS NEW OWNERS, a Rottweiler puppy had a blast—one big enough to destroy the house.

Paula Dodson and her family had gone out for the day and left their three-month-old puppy Jake alone at their Norman, Oklahoma, house on March 30, 2001. When they returned, they were shocked to see that their home had turned to rubble. An explosion had blown the roof six inches off the house and collapsed several brick walls.

Almost as shocking was their discovery that Jake was alive in the middle of all the debris and had sustained only minor injuries. "I can't believe it, and even our vet can't believe it," Dodson told reporters.

Firefighters speculate that Jake was playing with a gas line switch in the utility room when it was inadvertently turned on, filling the room with natural gas. When the hot water tank switched on, the spark apparently ignited the gas, causing the violent explosion.

IN HARTFORD, CONNECTICUT, in the 1880s, many residents complained about the organ grinders whose loud music disturbed the peace on quiet neighborhood streets.

However, because the roaming musicians were not doing anything illegal, there was little that their detractors could do. It took the smarts of a dog to do what humans couldn't—drive the organ grinders out of town.

According to an article in the *New York Times* dated April 18, 1885, an unnamed mutt belonging to a resident who despised the musicians felt the same way as his master.

"However much the Hartford dog may have yearned for organ grinders' legs, he restrained the natural yearning and devised a method of suppressing organ grinders which would not involve his master in [any legal] difficulties," the article said.

"In accordance with a carefully matured purpose, the dog lay in wait in the front yard, and as soon as an organ grinder appeared and turned his instrument loose, the dog began a prolonged and melancholy howl. Not only did the howl overpower the strains of the organ, but it lacerated the tuneful ear of the musician, and after a heroic struggle, lasting nearly two minutes . . . the organ grinder retreated.

"The dog followed him, and when the musician reached the next block and again tried to play 'Sweet Violets,' the melancholy howl broke out close behind him. That inestimable dog followed his victim for an entire day, and finally drove him out of Hartford without permitting him to finish a single tune.

"Since then, the dog has never failed to howl down every organ grinder who has visited Hartford. His howl, by dint of careful culture, has grown more and more harrowing. It now puts the strongest organ grinder to flight in twenty-three seconds, and whereas two years ago there were at least twenty cases of organ grinding in Hartford every day during the summer . . . the noble dog has virtually purged the town of organ grinders, and he has accomplished this without . . . wounding a leg."

The article then asked, "Why should not all our dogs be trained to howl on hearing a hand organ? . . . It would not be six months before the hand organ would be driven out of the country never to return."

MOLLI THE BEAGLE had been a top dog for three years—because she spent most of her time on the roof of her owners' garage.

By sitting up there and watching the cars and trucks go past her, Molli became something of a celebrity in a rural neighborhood of Keysville, south of Plant City, Florida. In fact, she was nicknamed Roof Dog. She always brought a smile to the regular drivers, including kids on their way to the high school down the street, and caused a double take for those who spotted her for the first time.

She had been following in the paw prints of her predecessor Coda, a black Labrador retriever owned by John and Shirley Raulerson. When they got the Lab in 1995, he eventually discovered a set of old stairs in the back of the family's garage that led to the flat roof, which at one time had been a sundeck. Coda liked to spend afternoons lounging on the roof.

"Coda would jump up and get an orange off the orange tree in the backyard and go up onto the roof and drop it down, hoping someone would play catch with her," Shirley said in a personal interview. "She developed heartworm and we knew she didn't have long to live so we got an eight-week-old beagle and named her Molli." It wasn't long before Coda taught Molli how to enjoy the high life. When Coda passed away in 2002, Molli took over as Roof Dog.

The garage roof became Molli's second home, so much so that she even slept there on some nights. Whenever Kaleigh and Bailey, the

Raulersons' children, ran across the front yard, Molli would run along with them, but eight feet above their heads.

Shirley said, "People would stop and say, 'Hey, do you know your dog is on the roof?' And we'd say, 'Yes, that's why she's called Roof Dog.'

"A deputy came banging on the door the other day at 7 a.m. and said, 'You have a dog on your roof.' I said, 'You must be new to the area because we've had a dog on the roof for about ten years.'"

MEGAN THE YELLOW LABRADOR RETRIEVER was old and had a touch of arthritis that made it difficult for her to climb from the floor to the bed. But that didn't stop her from performing a high-rise stunt that froze one of the busiest sections of midtown Manhattan in October 2000.

"I returned from work to find the lobby of my apartment building swarming with cops—not just any cops, but New York's elite Emergency

Services Unit," the dog's owner, Mike Santangelo, recalled in a personal interview. "These are the guys trained to deal with terrorists, bombs, riots, hostage situations, and drug-crazed maniacs running around the streets with machetes.

"Officers with ropes and nets were scurrying from the street into the elevators of my building. Living a half block from the United Nations, I thought it could be anything—even an incident with implications for world peace.

"I asked the doorman, Ayman Abdou, what was going on. He said, 'There's a dog out on an air conditioner.'"

Abdou said that about an hour earlier, people across the street at the Ford Foundation and the Israeli Embassy, both of which faced the apartment building, were pointing to a dog crouched nervously on an air conditioning unit on the fifteenth floor. Many had called 911 pleading for police to rescue the frightened animal.

Although Santangelo lived on the fifteenth floor, he discarded the notion that the dog was

Megan because she was well-behaved, mature, and too old and weak for such hijinks. Besides, he figured, the weight of a fifty-five pound dog would likely have sent the air conditioner plunging to the ground. He assumed it was someone else's dog—a small one—that got out the window.

Santangelo rode the elevator up to his studio apartment on the fifteenth floor and opened the door. "I called out to Megan, expecting to see her wildly wagging yellow tail," he recalled. "But there was no Megan, no wagging tail. Just a nose—and it was sticking out from behind the closed venetian blinds covering the open window. I dashed across the room, stuck my hand out the window, grabbed the dog's collar, and hauled her back inside. Her ears were plastered against her head and she was shaking.

"As her feet hit the floor, an ESU sergeant stormed through my door, which was still open. He bellowed, 'Did you put that dog out there?' He looked like he was ready to stomp me as two other angry officers loomed up behind him. I told him, 'No, I just got home from work. I can't believe she got out there.' The sergeant looked unconvinced until, luckily, another tenant confirmed my story."

The sergeant huffed in disgust, spun around, and stalked out to collect his men who were stationed on the fourteenth and sixteenth floors, preparing to execute an elaborate rescue, Santangelo said. ESU members were afraid that the dog would get scared and jump if they busted down the door. So they planned to snatch the perched pooch from the apartment directly above her by rappelling down the side of the building after setting up a net outside the apartment below her in case she fell. But Santangelo's arrival averted their rescue attempt.

After the ESU officers gathered their equipment and left, Santangelo tried to figure out how Megan got out on the air conditioner. There was a high table, stacked with papers and books in front of the window. On the right was a chest of drawers covered with knickknacks and papers. To the left was a file cabinet with more papers and bric-a-brac, and a row of potted geraniums was on the inner windowsill. "But not a thing was disturbed—not a paper out of place, not a knick-knack upended, not a petal off the geraniums," he said. "I'll never know how or why she did it.

"Perhaps she had gotten lonely waiting for me to come home and gone to look for me. She had been living with me for only a few months after years of living in the suburbs. There, an open window or door always took her into the backyard. Having lived all her life where buildings are no more than two stories, there was no way she could conceive of a home fifteen stories above ground."

From then on, Santangelo made sure to close the windows whenever he left the apartment. But it didn't matter, because Megan never went near the windows again.

Tail-Waggers

IN AN INCREDIBLE EXAMPLE of a caring canine, a German shepherd mix has acted as a guide dog for a blind lapdog ever since they were strays.

No one knows where the pair came from or when they formed their friendship. They showed up in a bustling neighborhood in Van Nuys, California, in 2001. Their feet sore and their fur matted, the two thirsty, hungry homeless pooches wandered along the curb of the street when residents noticed something remarkable. The larger dog was carefully nudging the smaller one away from oncoming traffic.

"It's the most amazing thing you've ever seen," Barbara Fiero told the Los Angeles *Daily News*. "The big one wasn't going to let the little one get hurt."

Fiero's neighbor June Malecek first spotted the two dogs—a male German shepherd–chow mix and a female Lhasa apso–shih tzu mix—and noticed that neither animal wore a collar or ID tag. They looked exhausted. "You could tell they had been walking for a while," Malecek told the *Daily News.* "Their tongues were hanging out and the big one, he seemed really weary."

She set out a bowl of water for the canine pair, but the big dog wouldn't go near it until Malecek backed away. Then he used his snout to guide the little dog to the bowl and let her drink first. As the dogs slurped away, Malecek summoned Fiero, an unabashed animal lover with a dog, five cats, and thirteen birds.

Fiero, who spoke in a low, soothing voice and was careful to keep a safe distance, eventually coaxed the tired, filthy dogs into her fenced-in backyard. They took up residence in the plastic igloo doghouse that belonged to Sparky, Fiero's Lhasa apso, who was kept inside the house to avoid any canine confrontations. She named the two strays Samson and Delilah. While Delilah napped inside the doghouse, Samson remained outside the entrance, keeping guard.

Without finding ID tags on them, Fiero didn't know who, if anyone, owned the dogs. Judging from what other witnesses said, the canines apparently had trekked several miles side by side. Fiero and Malecek couldn't tell if the dogs once lived together, or struck up a friendship as they wandered the streets.

Fiero took the dogs to the vet for a checkup. It was obvious Delilah was blind because her eyes were clouded by cataracts and ringed by dark layers of rheum. She also suffered from ear mites. Samson was in better shape, although his black and beige coat was dull and dirty. The vet said there were no ID chips implanted beneath their skin that would identify their owners.

Fiero was delighted to adopt the dogs. She eventually gained Samson's trust so she could pick up and carry Delilah around the backyard. But the big dog never went far away, walking next to Fiero's feet as she held Delilah. Sometimes Samson rose on his hind legs to get a better view of his canine companion. He remained wary of strangers, watching them closely and giving a few deep barks if anyone other than Fiero or Malecek approached.

Ever since Fiero adopted them, Samson has continued to act as Delilah's guide dog. He still keeps his little pal in sight, checking on her constantly and standing guard when strangers are around. But he's mellowed a bit. "He'll let Delilah sit by herself on the couch," Fiero said. "He just lies on a pillow nearby with his paws in the air."

Unlike the biblical story, this Samson has remained devoted to his Delilah. Watching the dogs walk around her yard, Fiero said, "They're some couple."

WITNESSES CLAIM THAT A PET DOG saved a newborn baby girl who had been dumped in a nearby Kenyan forest to die—and carried her

across a busy road and through a barbed wire
fence to shelter in a shed.

The mud-splattered two-week-old baby
was found on May 6, 2005, after two children
reported hearing an infant's cries near a wood
and corrugated tin shack in a compound in a
poverty-stricken section on the outskirts of
Nairobi. "Two of my children, Colins and
Kennedy, came running to say there was a baby
crying in the compound but they could not trace
it," housewife Mary Adhiambo told the *Daily
Nation* newspaper. "I followed them outside and
we started looking around the compound and a
nearby plot. I saw my dog, which I have had
for the last five years, lying protectively with a
puppy. They were beside a soiled baby who was
wrapped in a torn black cloth."

The unnamed, tan, mixed-breed dog had
recently given birth to a litter (all of which
eventually died), and lived in the shack with two
other dogs who paid little attention to the infant.

The dog reportedly dragged the baby, who
was wrapped in a bag, across a busy road from the

Ngong Forest and through some barbed wire to the shed.

"I saw a dog carrying a baby wrapped in a black dirty cloth as it crossed the road," neighbor Stephen Thoya told the newspaper. "I was shocked at first, and when I tried to get a closer look, the dog ran through the fence and disappeared along a dirt road."

Adhiambo said she used warm water to wash the baby, cleaned the umbilical cord with rubbing alcohol, dressed her in fresh clothes, and fed her. She and her neighbors then brought the infant to a nearby police station before taking her to the Kenyatta National Hospital.

The seven-pound, four-ounce infant, nicknamed "Angel" by medical workers, was in remarkably good shape, hospital spokesperson Hannah Gakuo told reporters. Doctors believe the baby had been abandoned about two days before the dog found her, said Gakuo. "She cried a lot during admission because her umbilical cord was infected."

Angel's story attracted worldwide publicity, triggering an outpouring of help. Catherine Gicheru, news editor of the *Daily Nation*, said her newspaper was swamped by calls from people in Japan, Venezuela, and South Africa who wanted to adopt her.

Within days of the discovery of Angel, police announced the arrest of a woman who was suspected of being the baby's mother.

Meanwhile, the mongrel, who had been nameless, was given special treatment by the Kenya Society for the Protection and Care of Animals (KSPCA). Chief Inspector Javan Aketsa said they named the dog "Mkombozi," a Kiswahili word for "savior." The agency vaccinated and dewormed the dog because, he said, "we strongly believe she saved a life and we have every reason to care for her also."

Jean Gilchrist, of the KSPCA, told reporters at the time, "She is a very streetwise dog, that is for sure. The other dogs in the compound did not look very well, but she is the fattest of them all. She obviously knows how to look after herself.

"She wasn't happy when we all poured into the compound. She decided to leave, but kids in the compound brought her back for a bath because she was full of ticks."

The short-haired mutt, who was heavy with milk from nursing, was possibly trying to care for the child because her puppies had died, said Gilchrist. "She reckoned it was a young animal and possibly wanted to bring it up," she said. "It has something to do with the canine-human bond. Other dogs might have just left the baby there to die. . . . She's obviously a very special dog."

The claims that the dog rescued an infant from a lonely death sparked debate among doctors when the baby was brought to the hospital for care. Some physicians dismissed the story while others believed that a female dog nursing puppies could have been driven by maternal instinct to save the child.

Government spokesman Alfred Mutua said, "This is a very interesting development. It is one of those amazing things that happens in life that defies human explanation."

DOGS HAVE THE REMARKABLE CAPACITY to draw people out of their shells, a talent Gus the Leonberger demonstrated with amazing results for one young man.

Gus is a champion show dog. But it is in his other role, as a therapy dog with the Baylor Hospital Animal Assisted Therapy Program in Dallas, Texas, where he really shines.

Leonbergers are uniquely suited to therapy work. The breed, which originated in Leonberg, Germany, was created to resemble the lion on the town's crest. Known as the "lion dogs of Germany," these giants are covered with soft golden brown fur and are as regal and imposing as the King of the Jungle—but they are gentle as lambs.

On May 5, 2003, the friendly 120-pound furry therapist, accompanied by his human partner Peggy Walker, had been padding from room to room, comforting patients by resting his head on the edge of their beds so they could reach over and pet him. When the team finished with their ward rounds, Gus and Peggy walked downstairs to the harder work—rehabilitation. There Gus often helped seriously injured children start the long slow process of learning to walk or talk again.

Gus's last patient on that spring day was a young man named Jerry who had suffered a devastating head injury in an accident. To the dismay of his family and therapists, Jerry didn't respond to anyone or anything; he just stared blankly ahead, fists clenched.

Gus sidled up to Jerry's wheelchair. The therapist took the boy's clenched hand, put it on the dog's head, then moved it around so he could feel the soft fur. "Suddenly his hand relaxed on Gus's head and the therapist got very excited," Peggy recalled in a personal interview. "Then he clenched his hand again—with a bunch of Gus's skin and fur in his hand. Gus rolled his eyes and stood there patiently while they gently pried the boy's hand loose from Gus's head."

True, it was a small gesture, but to Jerry's family and therapists, who had failed to get any kind of response from him, it was a cause for celebration. Gus had somehow managed to reach him.

When the therapist put Jerry's hand on Gus's head for another try, the boy again grabbed onto the dog's fur and held tight. This time, after the therapists pried the clenched fist loose, Gus reached up and gently licked Jerry's face. Amazingly, the boy turned his attention to the dog. The therapist repeated the exercise until Jerry's face was wet with big sloppy dog kisses.

Peggy took Gus outside for a short break and returned with an idea. Dried mango ranked high on the list of Gus's favorite treats. So Peggy took a small piece of the fruit and put it between the thumb and forefinger of Jerry's clenched fist.

Gus reached over and gently took the prize from the boy's hand. After a few repetitions, Jerry started reaching for the treat and holding it out for Gus. Sometimes Jerry didn't hold it out far enough for the dog to reach it, so Gus would put one foot at a time on Jerry's wheelchair tray and take the treat.

Gus went home a happy dog, having spent the afternoon dining on his favorite tidbits. But he wasn't the only one smiling that night. "The therapists were over the moon," Peggy recalled. "Jerry's relatives were practically in tears with joy."

As small as these responses were, they were what everyone had been praying for—the first sign that Jerry could be reached.

It was with enormous pride that Peggy and Gus watched Jerry walk out of rehab a few weeks later. "Quite a miracle," Peggy said. "And Gus is the one who started the whole process."

IN ONE OF THE ODDEST PAIRINGS in the animal kingdom, a German shepherd puppy became friends with a wild barn owl—and saved its life when it became trapped.

In 1904, deep in the woods of Maine, trapper and hunter Dick Bruce adopted an orphaned pup and named him Pete. The dog was easy to train and possessed a loving, sweet nature. But it was still mystifying to his owner when Pete seemed to bond with a wild barn owl. At night, the bird would land by the dog and hop around while Pete playfully leaped at it, making sure never to catch it or harm it.

According to a story in the *New York American* dated December 31, 1905, "The attachment between the two grew as time went on, and it wasn't long before Pete began to disappear after meals. It eventually developed that he ate what he wanted and carried the remainder to points in the forest where he would leave it for his winged partner to dispose of when the coast was clear."

Bruce told the reporter that he thought about shooting the owl because of the racket it made at night, but when he realized how much Pete enjoyed the bird's company, the hunter couldn't kill it.

"The old varmint continued to hoot and saw away nights," Bruce said, "but I got used to it after a fashion, and concluded to let the pair go their own way.

"I would see them every now and then fussing around in the woods, but the moment the old owl laid eyes on me, she would dig out of sight so fast that there was no getting a bead on her if I wanted to.

"The pair had a habit of getting together on moonlit nights and raising a fearful racket. The owl would perch on a stump and hoot and the pup would sit at the base and howl. The more she hooted, the more he howled, and it would rile me until I got to thinking of the funny side, when I'd laugh."

But then the owl disappeared, or at least Bruce never saw or heard it for several nights. "I didn't think much of it until the pup got to staying away pretty much all night," Bruce recalled. "He would sneak off when he thought I was asleep, and a couple of times he stayed out until daylight. One morning he didn't get in until nearly noon, and I thought I would investigate.

"So the next night, after a light snow had fallen, I watched Pete. After I was supposed to be asleep, he dug up a piece of venison and off he trotted. I waited fifteen minutes and followed. It was easy following the trail in the moonlight, and after I had gone about two miles I heard a sort of low, hooting cry and then whines. I crept forward carefully, and there, in a little open space, close to Silver

Brook, was Pete lying with his nose between his paws, watching the owl devour the venison.

"I didn't quite catch the meaning of it at first, but I soon saw that the owl had been caught in a mink trap I had set the year before and forgotten about. That pup had probably been feeding the owl ever since its foot got nipped.

"The pup cried like a baby and his partner was scared most to death when I unsprung the trap, but when they found I meant the owl no harm, they quieted down. Since then, the owl has been quite friendly. Her leg will get well, but she'll always be lame."

For Thirteen years, Geisha Girl the shih tzu had wanted to be a mother. Every year, after being in heat, she would take her stuffed dog to bed with her, wrap herself around it, and baby it for several weeks.

Finally, in November 2004, Geisha Girl's dream came true. She became a mother—to two kittens.

It happened after her owner, Jean Schirf, of Edwardsburg, Michigan, heard mewing coming from the woods behind her house. Jean soon discovered a pair of two-week-old abandoned kittens that apparently had been left to die. She took the orphans, a gray male and a gray and white female, into the house and put them on the kitchen floor.

When Geisha Girl spotted the two tiny felines, her maternal instincts kicked in. She immediately began licking their faces and cleaning their fur. So Jean placed the kittens into the dog's basket to see what would happen. Geisha Girl cuddled them all night long.

Incredibly, a few days later, she actually began to lactate and nurse the kittens.

But because of Geisha Girl's age and the fact that she wasn't pregnant, she couldn't produce enough milk to satisfy the kittens. So Jean supplemented their diet by bottle-feeding them 2 percent cow's milk every four hours.

The dog, which the Schirfs bought from a pet store in 1991, never was spayed or bred. She went into heat about four weeks before she adopted the kittens.

It's not unusual for such dogs to sometimes have a false pregnancy and exhibit all the signs of being pregnant except for having puppies, Dr. Michael Lampen, a veterinarian with the Bergman Animal Hospital in Cassopolis, told the *South Bend (IN) Tribune*. "They will come into milk and the whole bit."

In Geisha Girl's case, "it was moderately accidental timing that this worked out for everybody," he said. "You have a dog with a false pregnancy and kittens who want a mother."

While the dog adored the kittens—who were given the names Dilly and Dally—the same couldn't be said for the Schirfs' other pet cats, Demi Moore and Jasmine. They were jealous, Jean said.

She and her husband Bill found homes for the kittens once they were weaned from Geisha Girl.

WHEN U.S. TROOPS entered the Baghdad Zoo a few weeks after they invaded the Iraqi capital, they were astonished to see dogs inside the cages of two lion cubs. But the canines weren't dinner for the cats. The dogs were their protectors.

The city's public zoo had been devastated not only by bombs and bullets but also by looting by Iraqi mobs who, in the aftermath of the invasion, stole most of the animals and left remaining creatures near starvation.

Wildlife officials gave a tour of the zoo to reporters in May 2003 and said that they had rescued several lions kept as pets by Saddam Hussein's eldest son Uday at a nearby presidential palace. That's where they came upon an amazing scene—dogs and lion cubs playing with each other. One large white mutt was acting like a surrogate mom.

"It's an amazing dog," said wildlife expert Lawrence Anthony. "If you go into the cages, she will protect the lions."

Anthony, a South African who was given the responsibility of helping nurse the zoo's remaining animals back to health, told the media, "We heard a report there were animals at Uday Hussein's section of the palace, and I saw two dogs inside the enclosure. We observed the relationship between the dogs and young lions and they were nuzzling each other. The female dog was mothering the young lions. I just couldn't believe it. They should have eaten the dogs, especially with the hunger they went through."

Officials of the zoo, located in the city's sprawling Zawra Park, decided to keep one of the female dogs with two of the three-month-old lions because when the animals were separated "they missed each other," Anthony said.

According to middle-east-online.com, Uday apparently raised his lions and dogs together so they could better protect his palace. He reportedly liked to enter nightclubs with one of his lions on a leash.

WHEN TWO NEWBORN LION CUBS were rejected by their mother, a fox terrier named Nell willingly adopted them—and even nursed them.

In April 1916, Spitfire, a lioness that used to be in Barnum & Bailey's Circus but was now living on a farm in Jersey City, New Jersey, gave birth to four cubs. But she refused to have anything to do with the babies and ignored their whimpers and cries to be fed.

"The poor little fellows just lay there and whimpered," Frederick Mitchell, co-owner of the farm, told the press later. "I decided we'd have to raise them by hand, and sent out for bottles and warm milk." He and his partner got the cubs out of the cage and tried feeding them through baby bottles. "They'd sniff and slobber over the nipples but we couldn't make them drink. It was no use. They were simply too young to take to the nipples no matter what we did."

Suddenly Mitchell had an inspiration. After bundling up the cubs, the owners took them to their Manhattan store, the Bartels Company, in the hope that their dogs Nell, a three-year-old fox terrier, and Georgiana, a hound dog, would become foster mothers. Both dogs had recently given birth to litters, although only one of Georgiana's pups had survived. Nevertheless, the dogs were still in the nursing mood, so Mitchell introduced two male cubs to Nell and the other two, a male and female, to Georgiana.

"Nell took to the little fellows," Mitchell said. "She had been moping in her pen, probably thinking of her dead puppies. At first, her back hair stood up and her eyes flashed, and for a second, we thought we'd have to jump in and save the cubs. Then she stepped gingerly over to them and sniffed them. She stepped back and growled. But her feminine curiosity was too much for her and she went up to them again.

"This time the little beggars did the right thing. They began groping about and whining pitifully like hungry puppies. That was all Nell needed. She looked at us as if to say, 'Why, they're hungry' and every bit of her ferocity and curiosity vanished. She just dropped down in the straw and adopted those little devils, who immediately acted like they'd reached home after a long and hungry journey. My partner and I knew that the future of half our cubs was settled."

Unfortunately, the two cubs that were given to Georgiana didn't survive the night because she refused to accept them.

Nell, though, proved to be a loving foster parent. She had only one problem with her cubs. Like puppies, they clawed and pushed with their front paws when they nursed, but unlike puppies, they had sharp claws. "They were scratching their new mother and punching her full of holes—abuse which she bore like a true mother, although she'd whimper now and then," Mitchell said.

Mitchell made leather mittens for their front paws so they no longer hurt their devoted foster mom. Nell nursed them long enough until they were able to drink from a baby bottle.

"What Nell did was one of the most extraordinary things I ever saw," Mitchell said.

A WEIMARANER SAVED THE LIVES of ten orphaned puppies when she took on the role of their surrogate mother.

Dog breeders Peter and Sharon Hardy, of Durham, England, were heartbroken when their five-year-old Rottweiler Emily died of liver failure after giving birth to ten puppies in November 2004.

Knowing almost all of the litter would die without a mother, the couple began to search for a surrogate parent. When dog lovers Gary and Karen Scobell, of Ashington, learned of the crisis, they decided to help even though they already had six grown dogs.

One of them, a twenty-month-old Weimaraner named Eve, had just given birth to her own litter of seven. The Scobells thought that she just might be willing to adopt and nurse ten more pups even though they were a different breed.

Because they were desperate and out of options, the Hardys brought over their helpless pups and introduced them to Eve. After a few sniffs, Eve began caring for the puppies as if they were her own, despite the obvious differences between Weimaraners and Rottweilers. "It is a bit of a strange mix, because they are such different breeds and we honestly didn't know if it would work, but they took to each other, which is lovely to see," Karen told the *Newcastle Journal* days later. "Eve has been treating them like her own puppies. It is really heartwarming to see them thriving. It's Eve who should be given the credit. She has taken to them really well and has so many hungry mouths to feed she is like a dairy cow.

"There is so much doom and gloom in the world, so to see a happy ending for once is wonderful."

Gary told the paper, "Eve has done absolutely fantastic. She is a lovely dog and to be a surrogate mum to ten puppies when she already has seven is amazing."

The Hardys were thrilled that the Scobells stepped forward. "It's really wonderful," Sharon said. "Gary and Karen have saved the lives of our puppies. We visited the puppies yesterday to see how they were getting on and it was absolutely amazing to see how Eve has taken to them. It is a real happy ending."

What's even more amazing, said Karen, is that Eve's mother was also a surrogate parent to an orphaned litter. "I guess it must run in the family."

"HERDING CATS" is a phrase that means an impossible task, too ridiculous to even consider trying. But that didn't matter to one abandoned chow chow who developed an unusual talent for herding kittens, earning her a spot in a cat lover's heart and home.

In 1995 L. J. Springer was a cat-care volunteer for New Yorkers for Companion Animals when the rescue group's director called one day and asked if she could make room for a chow chow. The dog had been chained to the door of a Brooklyn pound in the middle of the night. She was in bad shape, skinny and stunted, due in part to a horrific tapeworm infection. But despite it all, the fluffy black dog seemed upbeat and friendly, odd for her breed, which is reputed to be cranky and aloof.

Springer brought the dog, whom she named Beauty, back to her home on Long Island where she fostered a dozen cats, giving them a place to stay and much needed TLC while they waited for new owners. She also fostered one or two dogs at a time. They stayed in the basement, where they had access to the yard through a back door. Cats ruled the rooms on the upper floors. That way, there was no chance the different animals would come face-to-face, or, more likely, fang-to-claw.

Although Beauty was an easygoing dog, no one seemed to want her. She had been adopted out but then abandoned a second time, so Springer took her in again.

"After she had been here for some time, I noticed that Beauty had developed an odd habit," Springer recalled in a personal interview. "At the end of each walk, she'd stop at the front door where the cats were and I'd tell her, 'No, you can't go in there.' Each time she paused and heard the word 'no,' Beauty looked so sad that I finally gave in."

Clutching the leash, Springer nervously led Beauty through the feline empire. Some of the cats puffed up and looked at the canine intruder with shock and dismay. Others froze, then stalked off with great indignation or scrambled to the highest spot they could reach. "It didn't matter because Beauty was as good as gold," Springer said.

In time, Beauty became a member of the cat-care team, following Springer and her pet-sitters as they fed and played with the foster felines.

One day, one of the cats slipped out of the room and dashed into the hallway, with Springer in hot pursuit. Beauty then charged after the kitten and Springer braced for a bloody scene. But nothing happened. Springer recalled, "Instead, Beauty got the kitty cornered, then looked up at me as if to say, 'I'm just trying to help.'"

After that, any time a foster cat gave Springer the slip, Beauty would be on the job, heading the cat off and herding it back. If she couldn't get the cat to return, she would corner it, then stand and wait for Springer.

Once Springer realized Beauty had no intention of hurting a hair on any cat's head, she started to teach the chow chow commands. Like a cowgirl and a cattle dog, Springer and Beauty worked as a team. The commands were a little odd, probably ones that no herding dog would recognize. "Fetch Kitty," for example, would send her into action, chasing, cornering, and sometimes nuzzling with her muzzle to convince the fugitive to return.

"Remarkably, Beauty has always been very gentle and unusually tolerant," Springer said. "She somehow understood—without being told—that she couldn't use her full weight or strength with the kittens.

"I've thought long and hard about why Beauty chose this odd job. It certainly wasn't instinctive. Chows are generally thought to be aggressive to small animals. Nor are they known to be particularly skilled at herding or retrieving." She said the only explanation is that the dog so desperately wanted a home that she would do anything, even override her basic instincts, to prove that she belonged. It worked. Springer stopped trying to find Beauty a new owner and adopted the dog herself.

Lifesavers

BIYOU, a faithful three-year-old Australian shepherd mix, pulled her disoriented mistress from an icy stream, revived her when she collapsed, and then helped her struggle back to her house.

According to the dog's owner, Lisa Parker, of Richmond Dale, Ohio, here is what happened:

On the frigid six-degree morning of January 3, 2001, Parker, the forty-two-year-old owner of a farm, discovered that her blind horse was missing. Although she was still recovering from an operation, Parker went out into the cold to find the mare and bring her safely home. About 200 yards away, Parker reached a frozen creek and saw that the horse had broken through the ice and was trapped chest-deep in the water.

Parker tried to reach the horse but then found herself in the same desperate situation when she plunged into the icy creek. The bone-numbing cold quickly disoriented the woman and made her breathing labored. She began yelling for help, but no one heard her. In fact, no one knew she was gone. But Biyou heard her and, unlike the other dogs on the farm, she raced down to the creek.

Seeing her mistress in desperate trouble, Biyou crept out onto the edge of the ice. Parker then pulled off her iced-over, waterlogged gloves and grasped the dog's fur on both sides of the neck. While Parker kicked in the water, Biyou slowly and powerfully backed up until she pulled the woman out of the creek.

Once she reached solid ground, Parker collapsed. Her three layers of icy, drenched clothes were draining what little warmth she had left in her body. Time was running out because hypothermia was setting in.

Biyou pawed her and licked her face to rouse her. The dog even pulled aggressively at her clothing. Breathing heavily and unable to keep her eyes focused, the woman struggled to her feet only to fall again and again. Biyou continued to tug, lick, and prod Parker forward. Instead of taking the regular path, which required Parker to climb up a steep bank, Biyou led the way using an easier trail that the farm dogs took from the creek. With the loyal canine's help, Parker finally made it back to her farmhouse and called for help.

Although Parker recovered quickly, her horse could not be saved and was destroyed.

Hailed a lifesaver, Biyou was named forty-sixth Skippy Dog Hero of the Year.

"Biyou saved my life several times that morning—by pulling me out of the water and by urging me to make it back to the house each time I didn't think I could go any further," Parker said. "If it hadn't been for her, I would have either drowned or froze to death. She is my hero and guardian angel."

EVEN THOUGH HE WAS OVERMATCHED, there was no way Blue, a two-year-old Australian blue heeler, was going to let a huge twelve-foot alligator attack his eighty-three-year-old mistress. So despite multiple bite wounds, the brave dog fended off the gator and saved the life of his owner.

On a muggy July evening in 2001, Ruth Gay, of Fort Myers Shores, Florida, decided to take a walk with her dog along a canal behind her house. While strolling along the bank, Ruth slipped in the wet grass and fell face-first so hard that she broke her nose and dislocated her shoulder. Unable to get up because of other injuries, the elderly woman managed to roll over and yell for help, but no one was nearby to hear her. Meanwhile, Blue laid by her side, giving her comfort as she petted him.

Suddenly, Blue growled and ran off into the darkness. Seconds later, Ruth heard hissing, snapping, and barking. The injured woman knew instantly that her cries for help had attracted one of the many alligators that lurked in the canal. Earlier in the day, she had spotted three gators, ranging in size from six to twelve feet, swimming in the canal near the house. Because of recent heavy rains, the water had reached the top of the bank.

Now Blue was trying to protect Ruth from a large gator that had climbed out of the water and was heading toward her. Ruth's heart sank because she figured that a fifty-pound dog was no match for a full-grown gator ten times his size.

Although she couldn't see in the darkness, she could hear Blue and the reptile fighting about twenty yards away from her. She winced every time she heard her valiant dog yelp because she knew it meant he had been bit. But Blue refused to let the gator get any closer to the helpless woman, even if it meant risking his life.

After several tense minutes, the fighting stopped and Blue returned to Ruth's side where he stood guard. But a short while later, he took off to once again do battle with the gator.

"I heard the alligator and Blue fighting," Ruth later told the Associated Press. "Blue was yelping and whining. I knew he was getting hurt. Then the fighting stopped and I thought Blue was dead."

But Blue wasn't dead, although he was badly hurt and suffering from more than two dozen bite wounds. Now that he had driven off the gator for the second time, Ruth's faithful dog lay in the grass, bleeding. When her daughter and son-in-law, Sylvia and Albert Gibson, arrived at the house more than an hour after the first attack, Blue managed to find the strength to run to their car and bark and jump. Understanding that he was trying to tell them something, they followed Blue who led them to his injured mistress.

"It wasn't until my daughter came home and I heard Blue barking that I realized he was still alive and that he saved me from the alligator," Ruth recalled.

The elderly woman was rushed to Lee Memorial Hospital where she remained for six weeks, recuperating from shoulder surgery. She made a complete recovery.

Meanwhile, Blue was taken to Suburban Animal Hospital. Veterinarian Dr. Terry Terlep said he treated the dog for more than thirty bite wounds. A three-inch gash in Blue's stomach had to be cleaned and stapled shut. The vet then put him on painkillers and antibiotics and sent him home where he made a full recovery. "It's amazing what an animal will do in a time of need," Dr. Terlep said. "He's a pretty brave dog."

Blue's bravery was so impressive that he was named the Heinz Pet Products Dog Hero of the Year in 2002. Patti Jo Lambert, spokeswoman for the Heinz award said, "In all forty-seven years of this program, we've never had a winner who fought an alligator."

WHEN THE WORLD TRADE CENTER was attacked by terrorists, two guide dogs—in separate heroic efforts—led their blind owners down more than seventy flights of stairs to safety just minutes before the towers collapsed.

Yellow Labrador retrievers Roselle and Salty helped their respective owners, Michael Hingson and Omar Rivera, down the smoke-filled, debris-strewn staircases crammed with panic-stricken workers . . . and never faltered. The dogs suppressed any selfish instinct for survival and instead stayed by their masters' side despite the overpowering stench of jet fuel, the splinters of glass, and ankle-high water . . . and never hesitated.

Hingson, fifty-one, worked on the seventy-eighth floor in the World Trade Center for Quantum ATL, which, ironically, made tape libraries that back up data for disaster recoveries. At 8:46 a.m. on September 11, 2001, Hingson was conducting a meeting while Roselle was sleeping comfortably under his desk. Suddenly the north tower shook from a horrific bang. He had no way of knowing that the explosion on the ninety-fifth floor was from the impact of the first of two hijacked commercial jetliners to slam into the World Trade Center. "The building seemed to tip, and then move back to the center," he recalled later at a National Guide Dog Conference. "Then someone discovered smoke and fire, and people began screaming."

After yelling for calm, Hingson made a quick call to his wife Karen to tell her that there had been an explosion and that he and Roselle were leaving the building.

"We got down the same way as everyone else did," said Hingson, who walked down the stairways in the flaming building with colleague David Frank. "The smell of jet fuel in the stairwell was distinct and often overwhelming. We ran into groups of frightened people who had stopped their descent in fear. David, Roselle, and I would stop and give them a hug and encouragement that we were all in this together and try and get them moving again.

"Roselle's guiding was absolutely superb. She guided and behaved as if going down seventy-eight flights of stairs was a normal occurrence. At times, we had to move over to the left side of the stairway in order to clear the way for burn victims and firemen. On those occasions, I held the banister with my left hand, and heeled Roselle with my right."

When they finally made it out more than an hour later, Hingson and Roselle followed Frank to his car, but just as they were preparing to get in and drive away, the south tower began to collapse, and they were on the run again, this time to a nearby subway station. Because of Hingson's blindness and Roselle's excellent guiding skills, the pair was able to shepherd those like Frank, who had been temporarily blinded by the cloud of dust and debris.

But the subway station didn't turn out to be the perfect refuge either, because the north tower collapsed, and for a third time, they were forced to scramble to safety.

"Roselle and I were able to get out because of the close bond between us," said Hingson, who has been blind since birth. "Was our escape miraculous? Perhaps, but only as miraculous as all the other escapes."

Soon after the attack, Hingson joined Guide Dogs for the Blind—the San Rafael, California, organization that trained Roselle— as their national public affairs representative, sharing his story and demonstrating the strength of the human-animal bond.

Such connectedness between man and dog was displayed at the World Trade Center at least one other time on that terrible day.

When the first plane crashed into the north tower, Omar Rivera, forty-three, a senior systems designer for the Port Authority, was sitting at his desk on the seventy-first floor.

Following the violent explosion, he heard a cacophony of computers and furnishings crashing to the floor, people screaming, and glass shattering. The blind man said a quick prayer, and then called his dog Salty to guide him through the commotion. "He was very nervous, but he didn't run away," he later told the *New York Times*.

With one hand on Salty's harness and the other on the arm of his supervisor, Donna Enright, Rivera descended into a crowded stairway filling with acrid smoke and smelling of jet fuel. Salty refused to leave his side, even when another coworker tried to take the dog's leash. Together, they kept pushing forward.

As he and Salty inched down the crowded stairs and over chunks of debris, Rivera heard crying, screaming, and praying from desperate men and women. He also heard walls cracking and floors buckling.

An hour and fifteen minutes later, Rivera and Salty came out on the ground floor. Although Salty was exhausted, they both kept walking. Then they broke into a run as the tower started to collapse. Salty remained obedient and loyal as he, Rivera, and Enright scrambled for safety ahead of the fast-moving debris cloud.

Rivera, who lost his sight to glaucoma fourteen years earlier, said he was able to focus on getting out because he wasn't distracted by having to see the destruction. "Not being able to see also allowed me to concentrate on asking God to please allow me to go back and hug my family," he said.

Salty was a graduate of Guiding Eyes for the Blind in Yorktown Heights, New York.

Both Roselle and Salty were honored by the British Guide Dogs for the Blind Association at an international conference in Texas and presented with specially made trophies. The association's chief executive, Geraldine Peacock, said, "Guide dogs are trained to look after their owners' needs and guide them through difficult situations, but this was clearly unprecedented and both dogs handled themselves with tremendous courage and devotion."

To PAM AND TROY SICA, their beloved golden
retriever Bullet couldn't have been a better
companion. For more than a decade, his gentle
nature and unconditional love helped get them
through a series of devastating heartaches from
Pam's six miscarriages.

In 2000, the Bellport, New York, couple
was dealt another emotional blow when their
thirteen-year-old dog became seriously ill and
was diagnosed with a bad heart condition
and a liver tumor the size of a softball. In a
personal interview, Pam recalled, "The vet
said, 'The dog is old and has a weak heart and
won't survive long. If we operate, we might
lose him on the table. It's your call.'" Because
of Bullet's advanced age, friends and family
recommended euthanasia. But the Sicas
wouldn't hear of it.

"We had Bullet since he was eight weeks
old," Pam said. "At that time, he was our only
baby. We scraped some money together and a
friend loaned us the rest so Bullet could have
the operation. People thought I was crazy."

Even though there was no guarantee that surgery would save him—the odds of survival were slim—the risky $5,000 operation proved successful, and Bullet returned home to once again help fill the void in the childless couple's life. "He came through with flying colors, much to the surprise of the vet and everyone else," Pam said.

Today the Sicas can only shudder to think about what would have happened had they listened to everyone and put Bullet down. They would have faced an unbearable tragedy. But that tragedy was averted because of the heroic actions of their old, loyal dog two years after surviving his medical crisis.

"I know now that there was a reason why I needed to save Bullet's life—because one day he would save my baby's life," said Pam.

The couple's joy over Bullet's recovery was surpassed only by their elation when, after years of trying, Pam carried a baby to full term and gave birth to their son Troy in 2002.

Nineteen days later, their happiness nearly turned to grief. About 4:30 a.m. on May 1, the forty-two-year-old mother was preparing a bottle for the baby when Bullet began barking uncontrollably. "He was jumping up and down and running around in circles, which was totally unlike him," Pam recalled. "I reached for his collar, thinking he wanted to go outside. He backed away and looked at me in an odd way and began racing between the kitchen and hallway. I followed Bullet to my room where the baby was sleeping.

"When I looked at Troy, I could hear he was having trouble breathing. Then his face went from red to blue and he was lifeless." Pam screamed for her husband, who began CPR while she called 911. Meanwhile, Bullet kept whining and remained next to the baby, who was now on the floor as Troy Sr. worked to keep him alive.

Paramedics arrived within minutes, but at first Bullet wouldn't let any stranger near the baby, forcing Pam to barricade the frantic dog in the kitchen. Paramedics revived little Troy before rushing him to the hospital where he was diagnosed with double pneumonia and put on a respirator. The doctors also discovered a previously undetected heart defect. Pam said that the paramedics told her that if they had arrived just two minutes later, her infant son could have died or suffered irreversible brain damage from lack of oxygen.

While Troy was in the hospital, Pam brought a photo of Bullet that she kept by the baby's crib. "When the nurses asked me why, I said, 'It's because Bullet is Troy's angel. If it wasn't for him, I wouldn't have a baby anymore.'"

Sixteen days after the crisis, little Troy made a full recovery and was allowed to go home. "When we got home, I put the baby on the floor and Bullet went up to him, nose to nose," Pam said. "The dog was so happy to see him."

During the first year of little Troy's life, Bullet was always by his side. "When I gave the baby a bath, Bullet was on the floor by the tub," said Pam. "If Troy was in the baby swing, Bullet had to be right under it. Bullet would sleep by the baby's bed. He would always kiss the baby good night."

For helping save Troy's life, Bullet was showered with awards. Among other citations, he was named Dog Hero of the Year by Kibbles 'n Bits and received the ProHeart Hero Award. "We truly believe that our decision to save Bullet's life saved our son," Pam said, upon accepting the awards. "We love them both. They are both our miracle angels."

The following year, Bullet's big heart finally gave out. "I've had dogs all of my life, but after Bullet, I just can't get another dog," Pam said in the interview two years after his death. "It's not time yet for me to get a replacement for him. How can you replace a dog like that?"

EVEN THOUGH SHE WAS IN THE HOUSE and her master was nearly half a mile away, Shannon the family dog knew that he was in serious trouble. So the seven-year-old border collie-golden

retriever mix bolted out the door and led the
man's wife to where her husband was pinned
underneath a tractor.

Ted and Peggy Mandry, both sixty-four, of
Washington, Missouri, owned an 80-acre farm.
On a June afternoon in 2004, Shannon was
napping alone inside their home. Peggy was
visiting some neighbors while Ted was on his
tractor, which had a front-end loader and a
mower on the back.

He had planned on mowing the hayfield,
but first he decided to take care of an erosion
problem in a ten-foot gully about half a mile
from the house. He parked the tractor and left
the engine running while he took care of some
brush—but the tractor popped out of gear and
rolled into the gully. Before Mandry could get out
of the way, the tractor tipped forward at a forty-
five-degree angle and the front-end loader
trapped his right leg.

"I was calling for help and whistling for two
hours, but no one knew where I was," he said in a
personal interview. "When Peggy returned home,

she just assumed that I was out mowing hay. She had no idea that I was in trouble. But Shannon seemed to know."

The dog was locked inside the house where the windows were closed and the air conditioner was on. Yet somehow she sensed, or heard, that her master was in distress.

"As soon as Peggy walked in the house, Shannon began acting strangely," Mandry said. "Normally, she's a well-behaved, quiet dog, but she began howling and scratching at the door. Peggy figured she just wanted to run with the tractor, so she ignored her."

When Shannon didn't get her way, her odd behavior escalated, and she started scratching wildly at the door—digging deep grooves in the door and the floor. "Peggy decided to put a leader on Shannon and take her outside and tie her to a tree," Mandry said. She attached one end of a rope to Shannon's collar and wrapped the other end around her arm. As soon as the door was opened, Shannon bolted, and Peggy had no choice but to run with her.

Shannon was whining and barking and dragged her perplexed mistress through the pasture and into the woods. The dog led her straight to her injured husband.

"I was bleeding and I was getting weaker," Mandry recalled. "I wondered if anyone would find me in time. I knew I was running out of time and that I would need a miracle to survive. At that point, my wife and dog arrived. I knew I would make it then."

Peggy rushed home and called 911. A rescue team arrived and spent an hour before freeing Mandry's leg. He was taken to a hospital where doctors had to amputate his leg above the knee. He now wears a prosthetic leg and is still able to drive a tractor but no longer performs heavy-duty work.

"While I was in the hospital, every morning when Peggy let Shannon out, the dog would run down to the gully to check to see if I was there," he said. "Once I returned home, she stopped doing that."

For her heroic act, Shannon was given the twenty-third annual National Hero Dog Award presented in 2005 by the Society for the Prevention of Cruelty to Animals in Los Angeles. The award goes to "a companion animal that's well-treated and has bonded with the family, so they somehow know what to do and step up to the plate when there's trouble," said Madeline Bernstein, president of the society's Los Angeles chapter.

Shannon was treated to a flight to Los Angeles—and sat in the cabin instead of being stowed in cargo—and stayed with her owners at a beachfront hotel. "The only problem was that she wouldn't drink the tap water there because she had been raised on well water," said Mandry. "We ended up having to use bottled spring water at $8 a bottle."

WHEN MASSIVE WAVES from the devastating 2004 tsunami were bearing down on the southern coast of India, a seven-year-old boy tried to hide in his house, which was in the path of a wall of water. But his faithful dog wouldn't let him and literally goaded him to safety—a heroic act that made headlines around the world.

About four years earlier, a relative gave the family a yellow mongrel as a present. The dog was named Selvakumar after another relative who had recently died. The dog was lovable, seldom barked, and let the owners' three boys climb on him and pull his tail without protest. Most days, the dog escorted seven-year-old Dinakaran to and from school in a village near Pondicherry, India, while spending the rest of the day playing with the boy's two younger brothers.

According to the Associated Press, here's what happened on that tragic day, December 26, 2004, when tsunamis killed more than 200,000 people:

Dinakaran's father, Ramakrishnan, (south Indians often use only one name) had just returned from the sea with a boat full of fish when he noticed that the tide was acting strange. When Ramakrishnan climbed to the roof of a two-story community center next to their home, he saw giant waves racing toward shore and shouted down to his wife Sangeeta to flee.

Sangeeta grabbed her two youngest children and ran for her life, figuring that Dinakaran could run on his own at least as fast as she could. But when she reached high ground, she realized to her grief that her son hadn't followed her. Sangeeta was devastated, believing she would never see him again. "I had heard from others that the wall of my house had collapsed, and I felt sure that my child had died," the twenty-four-year-old mother later told a reporter.

As the tsunami roared ashore, Dinakaran had run to the safest place he knew—the family's small, concrete-walled hut just forty yards from shore. But sensing danger, his dog ran into the hut after the boy. As water began to swirl in the house, Selvakumar nipped and nudged the boy to get him out of the house and up a nearby hill.

"That dog grabbed me by the collar of my shirt," Dinakaran later told the Associated Press. "He dragged me out." The boy said Selvakumar saved his life.

Sangeeta said she wept with joy when she saw her son walking up to her, with Selvakumar by his side. Believing some special spirit resides in the canine, Sangeeta declared, "That dog is my god."

A VALIANT DOG picked up an ignited firecracker to save a little girl from being hurt—only to have it explode in his mouth.

Bruno, an eleven-year-old Staffordshire bull terrier–Labrador mix, rushed to the rescue when eighteen-month-old Anne Marie McMullen

crawled to pick up the live firecracker that
someone had hurled over her backyard wall in
Belfast, Ireland, on September 13, 1996.

The gallant family dog knocked the toddler
aside and grabbed the explosive. But it blew up
in his mouth before he could drop it somewhere
safe.

"We were all in tears," the little girl's father,
Brian McMullen, told the *London Mirror*.
"Smoke was pouring from his mouth and there
was blood trickling from his nose.

"He was lying on his back, paws in the air,
eyes glazed and quivering all over. I was sure he
was a goner."

The family took the injured dog to veterinarian Peter Miller, who said, "He must have a
heart like a lion."

After the vet patched up Bruno's shattered
mouth, the dog, his tongue full of blisters, struggled back to his feet and walked home with his
relieved family.

"I've never seen such courage," McMullen
said. "Kids here are always throwing fireworks

and he generally runs away from them. But this time he saw Anne Marie was in danger."

Remarkably, this wasn't the first time that Bruno was hurt by an explosive. Several years earlier, he survived a bomb blast during sectarian violence in Northern Ireland. "Bruno's hind legs were badly hurt a few years ago when a bomb blew in our back wall," McMullen told the *Mirror*. "He's a brave dog. And he proved it again today.

"We had to spend our family allowance money to pay the vet, but Bruno is worth it."

WHEN THEIR CHILDREN FOUND A STRAY, hungry puppy and brought him home, their parents, Pat Picard and Lisa Trevino, weren't too thrilled. After all, the family already had four other dogs. But the couple let the kids keep him after they fell in love with the cute dingo and named him Tip.

Two months later, Tip rewarded their kindness in a big way. He saved the life of their three-year-old daughter, Aiyana Picard, when she wandered off on a cold night into the wooded hills of the Colville Indian Reservation in northern Washington.

At the family's rural home near the town of Nespelem, Picard checked on his daughter shortly before dark on August 6, 2002, and saw that she was watching the animated movie *101 Dalmatians* in her room. He looked in again about an hour later and discovered she was gone, along with all five family dogs.

Picard immediately called the tribal police who launched a massive search for the missing girl. She was wearing a T-shirt and shorts—not nearly warm enough to protect the toddler on a night when the temperature was dipping into the low forties. Authorities knew that if they didn't find her soon, she could die from exposure. To make matters even more serious, bears and cougars roamed the countryside.

Hours after the tot disappeared, all the dogs returned home one by one, but not Tip. The search, which involved 150 people, went on through the night and into the morning without any sign of Aiyana or the dingo.

"At one point, one of the men shot and killed a black bear a mile from our house," Lisa told *Woman's Day* magazine. "By morning, the trackers were talking about the worst-case scenario—that Aiyana might not be found alive. I refused to think that way and just kept praying."

Later that day—seventeen hours after Aiyana had disappeared—searcher Skumheist Jack spotted Tip deep in the woods covered in leaves and draped over the naked toddler like a blanket. "I was just getting ready to come down for lunch, and a little dog popped its head up," Jack told the Associated Press. "And there was the little girl, sitting under him."

Aiyana had walked about two miles from her home, and somehow had lost all her clothes along the way. When she got tired and cold, she curled up on the ground, but Tip kept her warm—and alive—by lying on top of her throughout the frosty night. He hadn't abandoned the little girl the way the other four dogs had.

"She'd been found less than one hundred yards from where the hunter killed the bear," Lisa recalled. "Not only did Tip save her with his body heat, but she wasn't even afraid because he was with her the whole time."

Tribal Police Chief Rory Gilliland said that thanks to Tip's devotion, the girl was in remarkably good condition, although she was a little dehydrated and had a few cuts.

Ever since the incident, Tip and Aiyana have been inseparable, said Lisa. "Tip even sleeps on her bed, lying across her chest the way he did when she was lost."

A CHOCOLATE LABRADOR RETRIEVER named Carly Simon had been an unwanted dog who had known little love in the first year of her life. But after Kathie Webber and her husband Chuck adopted the dog, she turned into a happy, loving pet.

And a lifesaver.

Days before Christmas, 2001, an unusual cold snap sent temperatures plunging into the twenties in Ocala, Florida. Webber wasn't used to the below-freezing weather, so she bundled up in jeans, an extra pair of socks, two sweaters, and a coat. She could hardly move from wearing all the bulky clothes when she went outside to cover her plants.

Carly Simon, who was named after the singer, watched Webber drape a sheet over her orange tree next to the pool, but then Webber slipped and plunged into the deep end. She sank quickly and was ten feet under the surface when her feet hit the bottom.

She tried to swim up, but she couldn't move because all the layers of clothing were soaked and weighed her down. She was standing upright, looking up at the surface, but there was nothing she could do to save herself.

"I remember thinking, 'I can't believe I'm going to drown here in my swimming pool,'" she recalled in a personal interview.

Just then Webber heard a loud yelp and saw a big splash above her. It was Carly Simon diving in. The dog circled around the woman's head for a few seconds, then stopped and dipped her hindquarters down so Webber could grip her tail.

Labrador retrievers like Carly Simon have strong, sturdy tails. Sometimes their tails get them in trouble, like when they sweep glasses off of coffee tables or knock children down. But that day, the dog was using her powerful tail as a lifeline to the person she loved.

Webber grabbed hold and Carly Simon started to swim with all her might, towing the drowning woman, who was rapidly running out of air. Although the dog was pulling about 200 pounds, she never stopped paddling. Slowly but surely, she dragged Webber to the shallow end of the pool until Webber was able to stick her head above the water and gulp in air. When Carly

Simon was sure her mistress was safe, she covered Webber's face with kisses.

Webber said later, "It was the best Christmas present I ever received."

ALTHOUGH TROOPER'S BACK LEGS were paralyzed, the German shepherd scaled a flight of stairs for the first time and summoned help after his elderly mistress had suffered a serious fall.

In 2004, the seven-year-old family dog suffered a severe spinal injury from an unknown cause that left his hindquarters paralyzed. After performing a two-and-a-half-hour operation on Trooper, the vet told owners Edith Tickner, her son Terry, and his wife Lesley that the dog would never regain movement of his back legs.

But it took the dog's love for Edith, ninety, to prove the vet wrong.

"His back half had been paralyzed," Lesley, of Addiscombe, Surrey, England, told the *South London Press*. "He could not even wag his tail and we had even looked into getting him a harness with wheels."

Just before Christmas, Trooper began showing limited use of his back legs. When he wanted to run, he put his back legs together like a kangaroo and half hobbled, half hopped around. But he couldn't climb the stairs—or so everyone thought.

Although Lesley and Terry lived in a big house with three children, Trooper had a special bond with Terry's mother Edith. "He has always been devoted to her," Lesley told the *Press*. "He follows her around the house. He only comes in the garden with us if he knows she is having a nap."

One night in June 2005, the family was asleep upstairs. Edith had trouble sleeping and came downstairs for something to eat, but she tripped and fell down the last few steps and was knocked unconscious. Hearing her fall, Trooper shuffled over to the elderly woman. "He looked at her and realized she was not going to get up," Lesley recalled. "He realized we couldn't hear her

because we had a fan on in our bedroom and our
door was closed."

Trooper knew he needed to get help for
Edith. Undaunted by his disability and spurred
on by his love for the woman, Trooper managed
to climb the stairs, push open the door to the
couple's bedroom, and bark until he woke them
up. Then he led them downstairs where they
found Edith.

Fortunately the dog's quick actions meant
Edith was left on the floor for only ten minutes.
Although bruised and shaken she was not seri-
ously injured from the fall.

"Edith could have been lying on the floor for
hours if it wasn't for Trooper," Lesley said. "He
is absolutely marvelous. We can't get over it. Big
dogs have such a bad reputation. Trooper's deter-
mination to look after Edith meant he overcame
his disability and his fears."

Wonderdogs

A GOLDEN RETRIEVER PUPPY who had been tied to a lamppost and abandoned was rescued and then blossomed into an amazingly special dog.

The pup was brought to the dog pound in Mount Holly, New Jersey, where staffers called Renée Herskowitz, a volunteer with the Burlington County Animal Alliance. It was her task to try to find homes for unwanted retrievers. According to a personal interview with Herskowitz, here's what happened next:

> When she first saw this pup in December 1999, Herskowitz didn't have much hope. He was filthy with fur like dirty straw and he acted like a wild animal. Worst of all,

the vet said the puppy had a weak heart
and would probably die in a year or two.

Believing no one would ever adopt
such a scraggly, unruly, sick dog, pound
officials told Herskowitz that they thought
it best to put him to sleep. That's when
she decided if no one else was going to
give the dog a break, she would. She
adopted the pup and named him Breeze.

Herskowitz had no idea that her dog
possessed a remarkable and rare talent.
All she knew was that they shared something in common. They both had medical
problems. Her doctors found that she had
a disease that weakens the body's nervous
system and causes seizures. There is no
cure, although there are treatments to
keep it under control.

Friends and relatives thought that
because she was sick, Herskowitz would
never be able to take care of a difficult
dog. But deep down she knew that she
had to try. First, she took the dog to a

specialist in canine heart problems who
gave her medicine for Breeze's condition.
Then she started training the dog, who
quickly became a well-behaved, eager
learner. With good food and loving care,
his coat turned from the color and texture
of yellow straw to golden silk.

They became best friends. But it
wasn't until early 2000 that she learned
just how much she needed him.

Herskowitz was downstairs in her
sunroom when Breeze flew through the
door and started barking loudly as if
saying, "Come with me!" She gently tried
to brush him away. Instead he grabbed her
pant leg and pulled her toward the door,
then up the stairs and into her bedroom,
where he pushed her down onto her
bed.

Seconds later, Herskowitz suffered her
first seizure. Had she stayed downstairs,
she might have fallen. Somehow Breeze
knew that. He knew that she was about to

faint and needed to get her up to her soft bed to prevent her from getting hurt.

At first no one believed her story about Breeze. Dogs can't tell when a person is about to have a seizure, they said. But scientists believe that some dogs have an inborn talent for predicting when a person is going to become sick. No one knows how, but the experts think that a dog's sensitive nose might sniff chemical changes in a person's body that happen just before heart attacks, strokes, and seizures.

Breeze, the dirty wild puppy that no one wanted, was one of these amazing dogs.

After that day Herskowitz continued to have seizures. Each time Breeze would warn her before they happened. Sometimes he would not let her leave the house because he knew a seizure was minutes away.

Meanwhile, Herskowitz kept training Breeze and soon he passed the tests to become a therapy dog, visiting old people in nursing homes and sick children in hospitals.

On Labor Day weekend, 2000—less than a year after the scraggly, unwanted puppy was dragged to the pound—Breeze officially became Herskowitz's service dog, with a snazzy vest to carry her medicines. Now he can go everywhere with her—to work and stores as well as to go on trains and planes. He's always by her side, ready to warn her of a seizure or to break her fall if she faints.

Herskowitz saved his life and now Breeze is saving hers. "He's my guardian angel," she says.

THEY CALL HIM MIRACLE.

Tortured and buried alive in a grave under a pile of huge rocks, the dog refused to die. Incredibly, he survived, and ever since his escape from death, he has touched the hearts of people everywhere—and, in some cases, changed their lives.

No wonder they call him Miracle.

If it hadn't been for his strong will to live, he would have died on an early spring day in 2000 without anyone ever knowing about it except his killer.

But on that day Nancy Marinchak, an animal control officer in Thompson, New York, investigated a report of mournful cries coming from a pile of large rocks behind a compound of bungalows. With the help of nearby residents, Marinchak cleared the mound and gazed upon a sickening sight. Underneath the rocks was an eight-week-old German shepherd mix puppy—bloody, bruised, and exhausted from hours of trying to claw out of a shallow grave.

A noose had been looped around his neck, and the other end was tied to a large rock at the bottom of the grave. It had been set up so that each time the puppy squirmed, the rope around his neck would tighten, choking him. Some sadist had obviously tried to kill the little black and tan pup. But the dog wouldn't die.

When animal rescuer Liz Keller heard about the injured pup, she rushed to the veterinary hospital where Marinchak had taken him. Even for Keller, who had two decades of experience rescuing abused dogs and cats, the puppy's injuries were horrifying, the most revolting case of cruelty she had ever seen.

Because of the strangulation attempt, the dog's eyes were bloodshot, the result of capillaries bursting from the pressure. His neck was swollen and his hind legs were temporarily paralyzed. He had a bump on his head, a fractured hip and leg, and bruises and cuts. From the level of dehydration, the vet estimated that the puppy had been in his grave for at least a day. Burns on his legs and terror in his eyes suggested that whoever had tried to strangle and crush the little canine had tortured him first.

Everyone at the animal clinic believed the puppy should be put to sleep. They figured that his injuries would take a long time to heal and he might never fully recover. Then there was the psychological issue. They doubted the dog would ever trust a human again.

But all thoughts of euthanasia vanished when Keller leaned over the puppy's stretcher and he did something that stunned her. He weakly wagged his tail and then he reached up and gave her a kiss.

At that moment, Keller, who founded the Glen Wild Animal Shelter a year earlier, decided that this dog deserved a second chance. And she was the one who was going to give it to him. "There was no way I could say 'no' to this little puppy," she recalled in a personal interview.

On the spot, Keller adopted him and authorized the vets to do whatever they needed to save his life, no matter what it cost. And then she gave him the name Miracle.

Keller understood that huge obstacles lay before them. For one thing, it would take thousands of dollars, which she didn't have, to patch up the physical wounds. And there was no telling how long it would take, if ever, before the puppy would stop cringing, whimpering, and urinating at the sight of a human being, especially older men who wore glasses.

But then the local newspaper, the *Times Herald Record*, put Miracle's story on the front page. The paper called him the "little dog that wouldn't die." As soon as the story ran, donations started pouring in. The post office had to set up a separate box to handle the avalanche of cards, letters, and checks—including a ball sent via overnight mail—for the puppy. Hundreds wrote in or called to offer him a home or just to find out how he was doing.

Within days, there was more than enough money to cover Miracle's vet bills. So Keller put the extra money into a fund to help defray the medical costs of other abused animals. She called it the Miracle Fund, which has since helped save the lives of dozens of abused dogs and cats.

The newspaper articles also spurred a rash of tips to investigators searching for the perpetrator. A caller told the cops that a kitchen worker in a local hotel had adopted a puppy who looked like Miracle but the dog was now missing. Following up on the tip, police arrested the suspect, sixty-two-year-old William Peoples. Keller was not surprised to learn that he wore glasses.

Peoples admitted the dog was his, but he claimed he wasn't being cruel to the puppy; he was attempting a mercy killing. He said the puppy had been struck by a golf cart and had been so badly hurt that he decided to put him out of his misery. But Miracle's injuries didn't jive with Peoples' account. Investigators discovered outstanding warrants on him from Pennsylvania, where he was wanted for several other offenses, including involuntary man-slaughter. In Miracle's case, Peoples pleaded guilty to aggravated cruelty and spent a year in jail. Then he was extradited to Pennsylvania to face more charges and time behind bars.

With a lot of love and care, Miracle's wounds healed and he blossomed into a handsome, strapping 100-pound dog. Despite his horrible beginnings, Miracle learned to trust most people, except older men in glasses. "He'll never forget the person who abused him," Keller explained.

The dog soon developed a special bond with children who easily returned his affection. This gave Keller an idea. With Miracle as the star, she created a program to teach children about the horrors of cruelty and the restorative power of love.

Today, Miracle and Keller visit elementary schools, pet shops, youth centers, and other places where they can get their message out. "We show the kids that if a hurt or traumatized animal or person is given a lot of love and kindness, they can recover," she said. "Good things can come out of a bad situation."

Sometimes the visits pay off in ways that Keller could never have imagined. For example, the team gave a presentation at a facility for abused children. "One teenage girl who was really moved by his story was petting him when she broke down," said Keller. The girl was crying so hard she had to be led out of the room and comforted.

Because the girl had never been willing to reveal much about the abuse she had suffered at home, she wasn't making much progress in therapy. But Miracle's visit changed that. "For the first time, she told the therapists what had happened to her at home," said Keller. "They never really knew." The girl finally revealed that her mother had tried to strangle her with an electric cord. The memory was too painful for the girl to confront, until she met Miracle who had been brutalized in a similar way. "From that point on, she did really well," said Keller.

"I think this dog was sent to me for a reason," Keller said. "There's just a special energy around him. He's just a great dog."

WHEN LEANA BEASLEY suffered an epileptic seizure and fell to the floor unconscious, her dog Faith knew exactly what to do. The specially-trained Rottweiler knocked the receiver off its cradle and with her nose speed-dialed 911. She barked repeatedly into the phone, and after a dispatcher sent help, the dog used her teeth to unlock the front door for the police.

Thanks to her training, Faith helped save the life of her mistress.

Because the forty-five-year-old disabled veteran is wheelchair bound and suffers from grand mal seizures, she has relied on a service dog for more than a decade. A Rottweiler mix named Bronson had been her faithful companion for ten years. She retired Bronson, but still kept him as a pet, after training Faith, a purebred Rottweiler, through the Assistance Dog Club of Puget Sound.

The dog, whose sensitive nose can detect changes in Beasley's body chemistry, knows how to alert her owner to impending seizures before they happen. Faith also has been trained to turn off light switches, flush the toilet, fetch medicine and other objects, and help Beasley with grocery shopping, dressing, and bathing.

On the night of September 7, 2004, Beasley was alone with her dogs at her home in Richland, Washington. That evening, Faith sensed something was wrong with Beasley but wasn't sure how to communicate the problem. The dog wouldn't let the woman out of her sight and acted strangely, like jumping up on the bed, which is a no-no.

"It's kind of hard to sleep when you've got an eighty-pound dog running around in circles on your bed," Beasley told the Associated Press. Wondering if there was someone outside, she got up and checked to make sure all the doors and windows were locked. She tried to go back to sleep, but Faith jumped on the bed again.

So Beasley went into the kitchen to make a cup of hot chocolate. She was reaching for the teakettle when she lost consciousness and fell out of her wheelchair, striking her head on the

counter before collapsing onto the floor. Faith
immediately ran to the phone and called 911.

At Benton County's Southeast Communica-
tions Center, 911 dispatcher Jenny Buchanan
answered the call. "I heard a dog barking and it
was very loud in a persistent manner," Buchanan
told reporters. "The dog was upset and sounded
like it was trying to tell me there was a problem
at the house." So Buchanan dispatched
Richland police officer Scott Morrell.

When Morrell arrived at the address, he saw
Faith and Bronson peering at him from Beasley's
front window. The door was unlocked and
Morrell entered the house. "Faith had already
opened the door for him," Beasley said. The dog
had been trained to recognize police officers, firefighters, and medical personnel as "special friends
with cookies."

Faith led the officer to Beasley, who was
sprawled motionless on the kitchen floor. After
paramedics were called, Faith remained by
Beasley's side and watched intently while they

tended to her. The dog tried to tell them that Beasley was about to have a seizure, but they didn't recognize her signal. Minutes later, Beasley went into convulsions.

She was hospitalized for three weeks, during which doctors determined her liver was not properly processing her medication for the seizures. "So my whole system was not working right," she said. That's why Faith was acting so strange. She knew something was wrong with her mistress but didn't know how to warn her, said Beasley.

Six weeks after the incident, Beasley, accompanied by her faithful service dog, met and thanked the people who helped save her life. Benton County Emergency Management held a ceremony to honor the amazing dog. "She's more than man's best friend," said Beasley. "She's a lifeline for me."

SOME SCIENTISTS AND CANCER SURVIVORS claim gifted dogs have detected cancer in humans.

Gill Lacey never paid much attention to the tiny mole on her leg. It just always seemed to be there. So she didn't worry about it when her dalmatian Trudii licked it one day in 1978. Lacey knew that Trudii was a food hound and she figured that the dog thought the mole was a spot of chocolate.

But Trudii didn't let up. "She started to pay unusual attention to the mole," Lacey said in a personal interview. Sometimes, Trudii would be strolling by, stop and sniff the air, and then zero in on her owner's leg. Lacey thought this was odd and troubling. "Her behavior was such that it made me think that what she was smelling was not something that she liked," said Lacey, who today works for the United Kingdom charity Hearing Dogs for Deaf People. "It was not a normal sniff."

She considered having it checked, but waited for months because she couldn't figure out how to explain the situation to a doctor. "It's such an absurd reason to go to a doctor," she said. But when Trudii kept sniffing the mole, Lacey finally decided to have it examined.

To the amazement of both patient and doctor, the biopsy showed that the mole was malignant, and it was the most deadly form of skin cancer—melanoma. Luckily for Lacey, Trudii had found it at such an early stage that it was easy to cure, simply by cutting it out.

"Trudii saved my life."

The remarkable canine nose has been put to use in all kinds of lifesaving activities, from tracking lost children, to flushing out criminals to sniffing bombs. But over the years, stories like Trudii's made scientists wonder if a "dog scan" could be as useful as a CAT scan in detecting human illness.

Dr. John Church, an orthopedic surgeon from Buckinghamshire, England, has had a long-standing interest in using animals, from maggots to rats to dogs, in medicine. He began keeping an eye on cases like Lacey's after a British medical journal published an article in 1989 about a border collie-Doberman mix that had, like Trudii, found a melanoma in its owner. The article also sparked interest among researchers in Florida, who trained an experienced bomb sniffer, a standard schnauzer named George, to distinguish cancerous tissue samples from normal ones. But the research in this area has moved slowly.

Finally in 2004, a group led by Dr. Church published the first study on the cancer-detecting potential of dogs. In the study, trainers at Hearing Dogs for Deaf People, taught six dogs—three spaniels, a Labrador retriever, a mutt, and a tiny papillon—to distinguish between urine samples from patients with bladder cancer and people who were healthy. The dogs got it right more than 40 percent of the time. It was not perfect, but it was certainly better than the 14 percent that could be expected with random chance.

However, the scientists were perplexed because all six dogs alerted to the urine sample from a volunteer whose lab results claimed he was healthy. But when the volunteer went for additional testing, his doctors discovered he had a cancerous tumor in his kidney that had gone undetected before the dogs found it.

After the study was published in the *British Medical Journal*, it received widespread publicity. Dr. Church started to get letters from other people who, like Gill Lacey, said their cancers had been detected by their dogs. In some cases, the dogs tried to bite the lesion off. This was enough to send their owners scurrying to the doctor.

One story stood out, Dr. Church said. It concerned a woman who walked around cradling her pet Chihuahua on her breast. One day, the dog started whining and pawing at her. When the dog wouldn't stop, the woman went to her doctor. A mammogram detected cancer hidden in her breast. After the woman had a mastectomy, her canine companion was still not satisfied, Dr. Church said, and continued to sniff at the spot. Thanks to her little pup's persistence, doctors found more cancerous cells, which might

have been overlooked until it was too late.
Fortunately, the remaining cancer was removed
in time to save the woman's life.

AFTER BEING INJURED, apparently by a car, an old
black Labrador retriever mix named Jasper knew
exactly what to do. He limped to the nearest
medical facility—a hospital for humans—and
checked himself in.

Not only that but after he was treated and
taken to a foster home for recovery, Jasper slipped
away and walked fifteen miles back home.

On the night of July 4, 2003, the thirteen-
year-old pooch hobbled up to the front sliding
glass doors at Beckley ARH Hospital in Beckley,
West Virginia. The canine triggered the motion
sensors that opened the doors, entered the
hospital, and then plopped down in the middle
of the hallway, waiting for someone to help him.

"It's the darnedest thing," Ted Weigel,
director of marketing and public relations, said

in a personal interview. "It was as if he seemed to know exactly where to go for help.

"At first he went unnoticed so he moved over to a spot where the admissions clerks could see him. When they realized he was hurt, they called Nancy Massey in housekeeping, who is a sweet animal lover, and she phoned Chris Vaught, the administrator on call, explaining that the dog needed a vet."

Although the dog couldn't show any proof of insurance or that he was anything other than a stray, staff members couldn't find it in their hearts to turn him away. "There was no way they were going to put an injured animal back on the street," Weigel said. "We're a nonprofit hospital and many of the people on staff are animal lovers, so the administrator approved taking some money out of petty cash. Nancy then took the dog to the vet for treatment."

Dr. Roger Ward, the veterinarian on call at the Beckley Veterinary Hospital, couldn't tell for sure what had happened to Jasper. He suffered some road burns and scrapes that indicated a car

had struck him. But the dog also had a pene-
trating trauma that caused a puncture wound in
one of his legs and it became infected, causing
him to limp.

"He was incredibly calm and patient," said
Dr. Ward. "He had a wonderful temperament."

For several days, the vet and Weigel tried to
find the owner of the dog, who had no collar,
tags, or microchip to identify him. "I put the
word out to the news media and the DJs picked it
up and the newspaper carried a story about the
dog that sought help in the hospital," said
Weigel.

When no one claimed the dog four days later,
Massey took the dog to her home in White Oak.
"I've had animals all my life, and I think this was
the sweetest dog I've ever seen," she told the
local *Register-Herald*. "He was so gentle and
good-natured. We just loved him."

Unable to keep Jasper inside her house,
Massey tethered him to a thirty-five-foot dog run
outside, where he instantly made friends with her
German shepherd. Her husband Ronald went out

several times during the evening to feed him dog treats and to play with him, she said. However, about 10 p.m., Ronald saw the Lab slip out of his collar and run away.

"My husband is disabled and couldn't go after him," Massey said. "When I got home, I looked for the dog until about 1:30 a.m. We left the porch light on, but he never came back."

That's because Jasper was heading back to his home in the town of Lanark, which is about eighteen miles from White Oak but only about a mile from the hospital. The following day he showed up in the backyard of his home, surprising owner Betty Ellison.

"I can't believe this whole thing," Ellison told the paper. "We were all really shocked on this one. To beat it all, it seems like he came back just in time for [her seventeen-year-old daughter] Christa's birthday."

Christa said that when she saw Jasper—her loyal canine since she was four years old—standing in her backyard, "I was tickled to death. I just couldn't believe it. He's my baby. Having him back is just the best thing that could have happened."

Because Jasper hadn't been neutered, the family was accustomed to his periodic absences and wasn't overly concerned when the dog disappeared. "We thought he probably went to find some place that was quiet because we had a lot of company over the Fourth and he didn't like a lot of noise," said Ellison. "We went looking for him but couldn't find him. He had gone away before, but he always came back."

They had no idea that Jasper had been injured and gone to the hospital for help. Not until the day before he returned home, when a neighbor showed them the newspaper story, did they realize what had happened to him.

"When we got the call from Betty Ellison that the dog was back home, we were really glad," said Weigel. "She was concerned about the medical bills, but I said we were happy to take care of it." He said the final tab was about $350.

News of Jasper's jaunt was picked up by the national wire services and made national TV news, including a live remote from Beckley on the *Today* show.

The adventure was somewhat costly for the dog, however, because while he was being treated at the animal clinic, he was neutered.

"It's amazing that this dog managed to find his way home," said Weigel. "That was a long way to walk and a pretty incredible feat. But then, this has turned out to be a pretty incredible dog."

PATRICK COFFEY RETURNED HOME with a nice four-pound, five-ounce black bass. But he didn't really catch it. His dog did.

As friends gathered around Coffey in the town restaurant in Bloomfield, New Jersey, on August 3, 1907, the angler hanged the bass, which was on a stringer, on a wall and told his story:

"I was fishing along the southern side of Oakes Pond without more than a weak strike every now and then. But I kept my eyes open, and pretty soon I saw something moving below the surface of the water about ten feet out."

Coffey was interrupted when Rover, his faithful Newfoundland who had been sitting by his side, began howling and then lunged for the bass hanging on the wall. The dog snatched the bass and ran with it out into the middle of the street, wagged his tail, and then returned to the restaurant, laying the fish at his master's feet.

"Gentlemen," said Coffey, "you see the antics of this intelligent animal. Now, I didn't want to tell you fellows the truth, not wishing to be met down as a nature faker. But my conscience and Rover have determined me. I must tell the truth, so here goes.

"What Rover did just now, he did this afternoon. Rover caught the fish. As I said, I was fishing when I saw something moving beneath the surface, and Rover saw it too. As we stood looking at it, this big bass leaped out of the water. Before it could get back in, Rover had leaped with one bound to the fish and caught it in his mouth. Then he swam back to me with the fish. That's the truth."

The story was told in the *New York Times* with a headline that read, "A Jersey Fish Story Corroborated by Mr. Coffey's Intelligent Rover."

TERRY THE FIREDOG was so smart he fetched his own dinner from a nearby butcher shop every day and brought it back to the firehouse before eating.

The dog, who made his home at a firehouse on Ferry Street in Boston, gained notoriety after a story about him appeared in the *Boston Daily*

Globe on December 22, 1889. Terry "has excited considerable attention of late for precociousness, vouched for by several persons," because of the way he gets his dinner, the article said.

"The firemen are in the habit of sending the dog for its own dinner, and every noon a tin pail is given to the animal, which takes it in its mouth by the handle and trots off to a butcher shop nearby. The butcher puts some meat in the pail, and the dog brings it back to the engine house before he touches a morsel of its savory contents."

But one day, when Terry arrived at the shop, the butcher was too busy with his customers to take care of the dog. "Terry sniffed and growled and clanked his pail about the floor," according to the article. "Becoming tired of waiting, he trotted back to the engine house with the empty pail.

"The firemen knew the dog too well to believe he had eaten his meat, and, concluding he had not been to the shop, sent him back. Presently, he returned again with the pail still empty, for it seems the butcher was still pressed with customers, and preferred to wait upon his two-legged ones before his four-legged one.

"The mystified firemen now told the dog to be off a third time and get his dinner. The dog stood still a moment, and then, as if a bright idea had just struck him, he was off like a flash without his pail. Presently he returned with a large slice of tenderloin in his jaws, and, wagging his tail furiously, as if at his own sagacity, proceeded to devour the meal.

"The firemen thought it was funny that the butcher should be so generous, but said nothing until a man came running up to the firehouse and declared the dog had rushed into his butcher shop and, watching his chance, had seized a slice of steak just as he placed it on the block."

Upon further questioning, the firemen learned what had happened: After being refused his meat at his regular shop, Terry had sneaked into another butcher shop and swiped the meat.

In the 1930s, Jack the fire dog was one of the most famous canines in New York City, yet he almost ended up in the gas chamber of the Brooklyn pound as just another stray.

Yet Jack was no mongrel. He came from an impressive bloodline of mascots. His father was a purebred setter at the Jamaican Race Track and his mother was a purebred dalmatian at Hook and Ladder Company 163 in Queens.

The dalmatian-setter mix was attached to Hook and Ladder Company 105 whose men considered him one of their own. At the scene of a fire, Jack would accompany the firefighters into a burning building and help lead them to safety if the smoke became too thick. At times, he would climb a ladder to deliver a tool in his mouth to a firefighter. He also could drag a fire hose if necessary.

When there was an alarm, Jack would listen to the sirens of other engines and could tell whether the 105 was going on a long run or a short run. That way, he knew whether to hop on the fire truck or to run alongside it.

But before the fire truck would get to the street, Jack performed one of his most important duties. Barking furiously outside the entrance of the firehouse, he would warn pedestrians and motorists to stay put. One day, a child walked right into the path of a fire truck as it was pulling out of the station. Jack leaped at the child, pushing her out of the way just in the nick of time. To honor him for this deed, the New York Anti-Vivisection Society gave the dog a medal on October 22, 1933, at a fete held at the Astor Hotel.

For all his remarkable achievements, Jack nearly faced the ignominy of a homeless mongrel's death in the gas chamber.

On April 13, 1934, he had wandered off and suffered the indignity of getting rounded up with several strays by the dogcatcher. Although he had a collar, it didn't have any tags that could identify him. As a result, he was considered a homeless mutt and was slated to be gassed in two days.

The day before the dog's scheduled execution, an observant attendant noticed a miniature badge on the collar that an earlier colleague had failed to see. The badge bore the letters "UFA," the initials for the Uniformed Firemen's Association—an organization that had given Jack membership in recognition of his abilities as a canine firefighter. The attendant called several firehouses in the area to see if any were missing a mascot.

After he called the 105, the firemen, many of whom had been searching the neighborhood for more than a day, were relieved to learn their dog was safe. Firefighter Frank Dowling raced down to the shelter to get their mascot.

The *New York Times* said, "What Dowling had to say to the dogcatcher, after Jack had leaped all over Dowling in enthusiastic welcome, would have delighted small boys everywhere."

Chowhounds

THERE WAS A REASON why Mark Meltz couldn't find the ring he was supposed to give to his bride on their wedding day. Their yellow Labrador retriever Liza had it—in her stomach.

The day before he was to marry Hillary Feinberg, Mark Meltz, of Peabody, Massachusetts, left the ring on the kitchen counter so he would remember to give it to his brother, who was to be the best man for the nuptials on September 4, 2000.

The next morning, Meltz didn't see the ring where he had left it. He assumed that his brother had taken it. He hadn't. And neither had his bride-to-be. It was shaping up to be a groom's

worst nightmare, and Meltz racked his brains over
what could have happened to the gold band.

He took the couple's one-and-a-half-year-
old Lab for a walk as he mulled over what to
do. When the dog began making weird coughs,
Meltz pieced together a possible scenario: The
cat jumped up on the counter, played with the
ring and knocked it to the floor where Liza came
by and swallowed it.

So on this hunch, the desperate groom-to-be
took the dog to Angell Memorial Animal Hospital
in Boston, where veterinarian Kathleen Wirth
took an X-ray of Liza's stomach. Sure enough,
there was the missing ring. To Meltz's dismay,
there was not enough time to operate and extract
the ring before the afternoon wedding.

What to do? Meltz's brother came up with the
solution: At the ceremony, he would substitute
the X-ray of the ring in Liza's stomach for the
real ring.

When it came time to exchange rings, the
bride gave him a wedding ring, and the groom

gave her the X-ray of the missing ring. No one else in attendance knew what was happening. "But once I explained it to everyone, they exploded with laughter," Meltz told the *Boston Herald*. Lucky for him, Hillary broke into laughter instead of tears.

While the newlyweds headed to Hawaii for their honeymoon, Meltz's parents agreed to keep an eye on Liza, expecting her to give up the ring in the traditional doggy way. After being fed a heaping portion of dog treats, Liza threw up, and out came the ring, right onto the Meltzes' rug.

FOR A COUPLE OF WORRISOME DAYS, Yazmin the beagle was a true watch dog—and it nearly killed her. That's because she swallowed a wristwatch and needed a life-saving operation.

Owner Jeanette Ben Nsir, of Condor Close, Droylsden, England, told the *Manchester News* in July 2003 that the family dog got her extra ticker by a freak accident. "My son Omar took Yazmin for a walk with a pocket full of biscuits because that is the only thing that will entice Yazmin back when she is off the leash. Unfortunately, Omar ran out of biscuits. He was holding the watch in his hand and Yazmin gulped it down, thinking it was a biscuit.

"Omar was very upset by what happened. We waited a couple of days hoping for nature to take its course, and when that didn't happen, we rushed her to the vet."

It now became a race against time because Yazmin was getting ill. Veterinarian Andrew Iveson, of Companion Care Vets in Tameside, took an X-ray that clearly showed the watch was still lodged in her stomach beneath her rib cage. "The consequences could have been grave," he said. "If the watch had blocked her intestine, it could have been fatal. We operated immediately. When we cut open her stomach and took the watch out, it was still ticking. She had six stitches and was able to go home to her family later the same day."

Yazmin made a full recovery and was back to her usual lively self again.

Iveson said dogs will gobble up anything they can get their paws on. "They tend to swallow some very strange things," he said. "I've taken everything from rubber balls and toy cars to a lady's G-string out of a dog's stomach. Nothing surprises me anymore."

IF EVER THERE WERE a canine sword-swallowing contest, Millie the Staffordshire bull terrier would be a strong favorite to win.

The two-year-old dog accidentally gulped down an entire stick only two inches shorter than her own body. Incredibly, she suffered no serious injuries.

According to the London *Daily Mail,* Millie was playing fetch with her owner John Hurst in a field behind his home in Portsmouth, England, in March 2005. Hurst threw a sixteen-inch stick for Millie to retrieve, but it stuck in the ground like a javelin. The sprinting dog dived on it mouth first and swallowed it whole, effectively impaling herself.

Fearing the worst, Hurst rushed his pet to a vet, where microcameras found the stick had somehow worked its way down Millie's throat and deep into her stomach. Miraculously, the stick didn't hit any vital organs. After a two-hour operation, the only injury to Millie was a small scratch inside her stomach.

Dogs receiving treatment for a swallowed stick is common, veterinarian Matthew Tyler told the newspaper. "But for a dog to get a stick stuck this far down is unheard of," he added.

MOST CANINES have a hankering for a bone. Not Charlie the bloodhound. He had a taste for a phone.

For Christmas 1998, Rachel Murray of Hendon, North London, England, bought her boyfriend Tony Dangerfield a Nokia cell phone from a company called Orange. She neatly wrapped it in holiday gift paper and placed it lovingly under the Christmas tree.

But shortly before the big day, the couple found that the present had been opened and wrapping paper had been torn and shredded everywhere. The box was empty. Suspicion immediately turned to Dangerfield's 120-pound dog Charlie.

Thinking that he had played with the phone and hidden it somewhere, Murray contacted Orange customer services, which gave her a number she could call to ring the lost Nokia in an effort to find it. She dialed the number and heard a faint ringing. When she traced the sound, she was perplexed because it seemed to be coming from *inside* the bloodhound.

"At first I thought Charlie was lying on the phone, and then I realized where it was," Murray told the *Birmingham Evening Mail*. "I couldn't believe he'd swallowed it. I sat there in disbelief."

But once she got over her shock, Murray recalled, "I couldn't stop laughing when I realized Charlie had eaten it."

The couple took the bloodhound to the animal clinic where the vet said that Charlie was big enough to be able to pass the small phone. The next day, after nature took its course, the Nokia emerged in perfect working order.

A STRAY MUTT nicknamed Broadway Joe was such a beggar that it almost killed him.

The likable, sociable mongrel—part terrier, part beagle, and part spaniel—appeared one day in downtown Troy, New York, in 1975. He had black and white splotches of short hair all over him and a pair of big sad eyes that made people feel sorry for him. Letter carriers, bartenders, storekeepers, waiters, and others began petting him and feeding him.

Because he spent most of his time sleeping and mooching handouts along a street named Broadway in Troy, his human pals started calling him Broadway Joe. Every day, he would amble down the street, stopping in front of every friendly face he saw. With those woeful eyes of his, he would gaze up at the person until the mutt was given a pork chop, some shrimp, or a piece of steak. Then he'd wag his tail in thanks and move on to the next soft-hearted dog lover.

One night, someone who didn't like canines lured Broadway Joe into a car and drove him five miles out of town and dropped him off. But by morning, the dog was back on Broadway, resuming his routine of begging outside places like a hotel, a barbershop, and a restaurant where patrons would offer him the leftovers they had put in doggie bags just for him.

Unfortunately, these people were killing him with kindness. One day, someone found the dog lying on his back on the sidewalk in obvious discomfort. Broadway Joe was rushed to a veterinarian who diagnosed the problem—the dog was suffering from a near-fatal kidney ailment caused by wolfing down too many fatty foods and not drinking enough water.

Although he came close to death, Broadway Joe pulled through after several days in the animal hospital. Rose Coon, who ran a beauty shop on Broadway, let the dog stay with her while he recovered—and kept him on a strict new diet.

When people found out that the dog was sick, they raised more than enough money to pay his $226 vet bill. "He's the only dog in this city with a bank account," Rose told the Associated Press at the time.

Before long, Broadway Joe was back on the street, but this time his real friends refused to feed him their leftovers. He had to eat regular dog food instead.

RUBIN THE LABRADOR RETRIEVER liked his mistress's sexy lace panties so much that he ended up in the operating room after swallowing a pair of them.

His owner, Josie Dubois, twenty-five, of Yeovil, Somerset, England, was perplexed when she found him choking and panting one day in June 2005. She rushed him to the veterinarian, who determined Rubin needed emergency surgery after discovering something soft in his stomach.

"I was so worried," Dubois told the *London Mirror*. "But when the vet came out of the [operating room] he was smirking. He asked me if I had lost any underwear. Then he showed me the pair of red knickers they had found in Rubin's stomach. I was so embarrassed.

"The vet asked if I wanted them back and I went bright red. I don't think I will be wearing them again."

Veterinarian Bill Petheram, who operated on Rubin, told the paper, "Dogs swallow knickers, stockings, and socks. They root through laundry as they like the smell. But if the foreign body is left inside the dog, the dog will die."

After receiving a vet bill of $437, which was covered by her pet insurance, Dubois said she will make sure her dog stays away from her laundry.

ALSO IN 2005, a veterinarian in Germany operated on a bull terrier named Breiti to remove a suspected stomach tumor—and found an undigested woman's G-string instead. Said Christiane Thul-Steinheuer, an animal-shelter worker in Troisdorf, Germany, "Bull terriers tend to have fetishes. Some like shoes, but with Breiti, it's lacy lingerie. To each his own."

LIBBY THE GERMAN SHEPHERD loved to fetch golf balls. But it soon became dangerously clear that she also loved swallowing them too.

When she became sick and was taken to the animal clinic, the vet determined that she needed an operation to extract the balls that were rattling around in her stomach. So before the surgery, the animal doctors made bets over the number of balls they would find. They weren't even close. They pulled out an astonishing twenty-eight golf balls!

The dog developed her penchant for golf balls in 2004 when Mike Wardrop, the bar manager at the Didsbury Golf Club in Manchester, England, brought his eighteen-month-old dog to the course. Wardrop watched with pride as Libby picked up balls on their daily walk around the links. She would often drop them at his feet, but little did he know that she was swallowing the rest.

"It got to the stage where she would pick up four or five balls every day," he told the BBC. "She loved fitting them in her mouth. She would bring them to me and I'd have a laugh. I had no idea she was wolfing them down as well."

Wardrop soon noticed that Libby had lost her appetite. When his wife Julie saw Libby coughing up blood, she rushed the dog to the nearby Greenbank Veterinary Clinic.

"The vets didn't even have to do an X-ray because they could hear the balls and feel them rattling around," said Wardrop. "They were having bets about how many would be in there. I think the highest bet was eleven, so they were shocked when twenty-eight came out. I find it hard to believe she swallowed them whole, and I'm gobsmacked to say the least."

Total, the balls weighed six pounds and were recovered during a two-and-a-half-hour operation. Libby needed thirty stitches to sew her back up. The medical bills totaled over $1,000, but Wardrop said it was worth every penny.

"Libby is fine now and a bit more bouncy than she was before. We've got every single ball back and we're keeping them as a memento." At roughly $36 a ball, it's a pretty expensive memento.

Now when he takes her out on the course to fetch a ball, it's a soccer ball. "I had to buy her two footballs," he said. "At least she can't swallow those."

It's UNLIKELY that any dog was more "stoned" than Belle.

The two-year-old springer spaniel had to undergo an emergency operation after she gobbled down more than 600 ornamental stones from the family's front yard in January 2002.

"I don't know what got into her that day, but the stones were blocking her intestines and she was doing very poorly," owner Margaret Westwood, of Halesowen near Birmingham, England, told the BBC.

Veterinarian Antonio Fratello said he had never seen anything like it in five years of practice. "She is definitely lucky to be alive," he said. "She had a stone blocking the intestine, and it was about to perforate it, which was very dangerous." He successfully removed about 400 stones from her stomach.

At first, no one knew that Belle had wolfed down the stones. The family was perplexed because so many of them were missing. Then one day Belle threw up more than 200 pebbles. That's when Westwood rushed her to the vet.

"Some of the stones were quite jagged and the worry was that she could have punctured her stomach lining," said a staffer at the animal clinic.

Of the ornamental stones that they knew Belle had eaten, the family counted 620. But they can't be sure how many others she had swallowed. The Westwoods removed the pebbles from their yard and replaced them with larger rocks too big to swallow.

TALK ABOUT HAIR OF THE DOG. A puppy swallowed a whole hairbrush.

When Leo, a four-month-old Staffordshire bull terrier, stopped eating in February 2005, his owner, Leanne Marston, of Llanrumney, Cardiff, Wales, took him to the People's Dispensary for Sick Animals. There, veterinarian Deborah Mir examined the pup and took him into surgery after feeling, through his skin, a solid object in his stomach. She didn't know what it was.

She operated almost immediately because, although Leo was not in any pain, the obstruction was too big to pass through on its own and could have ruptured his bowel.

The vet made one large cut to open the lower abdomen and saw that Leo had swallowed a five-inch-long hairbrush. But when Dr. Mir tried to remove it, she realized it was connected by knots of hair that had twisted around Leo's bowel. She had to make four more smaller incisions to untangle the hair and pull out the offending object.

The vet told the BBC that Leo's gut had burst at one point, giving him peritonitis, a serious inflammation. "I've seen tights, balls, bones, and string swallowed, but never a hairbrush," Dr. Mir said.

His owner was shocked when she learned what the dog had gobbled. "I couldn't believe it—a hairbrush of all things," Marston said.

"I've got three daughters so it could have been any of ours."

Leo surprised everyone by making a speedy recovery and was back to his usual self within a day.

A PUPPY that liked to swallow live critters got more than a bellyful.

Ariel, a German shepherd–Lab mix, prowled the backyard of her home in Fonda, New York, in search of fresh munchies—the kind that's still breathing when it goes down her gullet. There were mice, voles, chipmunks, and other small creatures, all quite tasty to a young dog. Even better, Ariel got to chase her between-meal snacks around the yard before she wolfed them down—fur, bones, teeth, and all.

Her owner, Joyce Rajkowski, didn't worry much about Ariel's penchant for backyard dining, until suppertime one hot summer day. As always, Ariel inhaled her regular dog food, but just a couple of minutes later, the dog became terribly sick.

"She was very nervous" Rajkowski said, "making that gagging noise dogs do when they chew on grass." Because these are signs of a possible serious condition, the owner was getting ready to call the veterinarian.

But her fears quickly disappeared when Ariel finally revealed what the problem was by throwing up on the rug. "Out came a whole rabbit—ugh," Rajkowski recalled. "It must have been the combination of the heat and overeating. Who knew she had just devoured an entire bunny?"

Survivors

COOPER THE GOLDEN RETRIEVER refused to be gator bait for an enormous alligator.

Despite being attacked by a reptile that was six times his weight and three times his size, the spirited dog somehow, some way fought off the monster and lived to bark another day.

"I thought he was dead," the dog's fourteen-year-old owner Chase Kierspe, of Pinopolis, South Carolina, said in a personal interview. "The alligator was huge. I didn't think he could fight it."

On a hot June afternoon in 2005, the five-year-old family pet, who loves to swim, managed to sneak out of the fenced-in backyard bordering a small channel that flows into Lake Moultrie. Chase was cutting the grass when he discovered that Cooper had paddled across the channel and was standing under a pine tree on the far bank.

Chase looked in the water beneath the pine and spotted the biggest alligator he'd ever seen. "I threw my drink cup and a lawn chair at it, hoping it would go away," said Chase. "But the gator didn't move." Then, to the teen's horror, Cooper leaped into the water to swim back home, totally unaware that the big gator was heading straight for him.

"I was yelling and screaming and running in circles," he said. "I screamed for help."

There was little that anyone could do. The gator attacked, and the dog fought back. The odds were against the retriever, but Cooper showed he was no ordinary dog. Cooper, who was snarling, growling, and biting, managed to escape from the ferocious reptile and scrambled safely to the bank.

He suffered several severe lacerations and lost a few teeth in his battle to survive. Flesh and muscle were torn from a front leg and chunks of skin were missing from both haunches. But he got in a few licks of his own because the gator, which chose not to pursue him on land, sustained several bites to its snout.

Wildlife officers later caught and destroyed the huge alligator, which weighed 740 pounds, stretched twelve feet from tip to tail, and was estimated to be about sixty years old. The state doesn't keep records of alligator size. But this gator "was certainly one of the largest, if not the largest, we've taken in some time," said Walt Rhodes of the South Carolina Department of Natural Resources.

Chase's father, Tom Kierspe, marveled at Cooper's ability to escape from the jaws of death. "I never heard of a dog getting away from an alligator in the water," he said. "You always hear that they grab them, go under, and do the 'death roll.'"

Cooper didn't seem all that fazed by the ordeal—either that or he didn't learn his lesson. "Every chance he gets, he tries to go in for a quick swim," said Chase.

IT'S PERFECTLY UNDERSTANDABLE why Sport the beagle hates thunderstorms after what happened to him.

His owner Sally Andis of Washington, Indiana, put the three-year-old dog outside in the yard as a storm rumbled in the distance. She clipped his collar to a chain that wrapped around a tree because Sport had a tendency to follow his nose into places where he didn't belong.

Suddenly, as Andis was standing near the back door, a bolt of lightning tore out of the sky and struck the tree. It zipped down the trunk, along the chain, into and out of Sport, and then traveled through the ground to her house, where it blew out the wiring of all the electrical appliances and blasted several bricks out of the wall, flinging them forty feet away.

"It was like dynamite going off," said Andis, recalling that day in April 2002. "I let out a holler and then I couldn't see anything. The sound was really loud, and I couldn't hear out of my right ear. I was so disoriented . . . Everything looked like it was in some kind of fog."

Andis, who was momentarily knocked out, said that when she regained her senses, Sport was gone. In a panic, she rushed to the tree that he had been under, but all she could find was a charred ring around the trunk, a melted chain, and three paw-shaped scorch marks on the ground.

Andis was certain that Sport could not have survived being hit by a lightning bolt, which can reach temperatures four times hotter than the surface of the sun and generate somewhere between 100 million to a billion volts. But the owner went looking for him anyway.

After a brief search, she found him down by the creek that runs behind her house. Sport was "smoking," she recalled. His coat was singed, some of the fur was gone, his paws were blistered and bleeding, and he smelled really bad. But his tail was still wagging.

"He's really a happy little dog," she said. And a really lucky one too. Very few dogs who are struck by lightning survive.

In fact, veterinarian Steven Marks, head of Small Animal Medicine at the University of Illinois Veterinary Medicine Teaching Hospital and an expert in the treatment of dogs that have suffered electric shocks, said he couldn't remember a single other case in scientific literature in which a dog survived a lightning strike.

Sport recovered from his burn injuries, thanks to some TLC and antibiotic cream. The only thing that's changed about him, Andis said, is that he appears a little more jumpy around loud noises, especially fireworks and thunderstorms.

ON AN AUGUST DAY IN 2003, an unwanted year-old basenji mix was put into the gas chamber with six other doomed dogs at the St. Louis city dog pound. Animal control supervisor Rosemary Ficken closed the door and pumped in the same kind of deadly carbon monoxide gas that had been used to kill 3,000 of the city's stray and abandoned animals every year.

Twenty minutes later, when Ficken opened the door to the death box, she was flabbergasted. There, standing on top of six dead dogs, was the reddish-brown mutt, groggy but very much alive, his tail wagging slightly. Never in the shelter's sixty-four-year history had a dog ever survived the chamber's noxious fumes.

Unwilling to close the door and re-gas the dog, Ficken believed the big-eared mutt deserved a second chance at life.

Ever since then, the death-defying dog has been a poster pup for the humane treatment of unwanted animals.

Until that fateful day, life was bleak for the basenji mix. Undernourished and unloved, he was turned over to the pound by an owner who no longer wanted him. When no one chose to adopt him, the mutt's time appeared up. He landed in the death chamber, but apparently he wasn't ready to die.

When Ficken saw that he was still alive after the gassing, she didn't have the nerve to kill him. So the dog was given a reprieve. The next morning, the dog was jumping up and down, wagging his tail, ready to play.

"There was a reason for this dog not to go down," said Rich Stevson, program manager for the city's animal center. "Maybe this dog is a special dog of some kind."

Ficken called Randy Grim, the founder of Stray Rescue of St. Louis. The organization rescues abused and neglected animals, restores them to health, and places them in new homes.

"She told me, 'Please, take him. I don't have the heart to put him back in there and re-gas him,'" Grim recalled. "To me, it's a miracle or divine intervention. I can't help but think he's here to serve a higher purpose. This case blew me away. This is amazing."

The survival tale brought headlines, television cameras, and more than 700 offers of adoption. "You can tell he's really digging it," Grim said at the time. "His bad days are behind him for good."

Grim adopted the pooch and named him Quentin after California's notorious San Quentin prison. "We feel like he beat the odds and escaped from a prison, of sorts." (For the record, San Quentin has its own death row and execution chamber, but it uses lethal injections rather than poison gas.)

Although Quentin's life was spared that day, many others are not so lucky. Ever since he was given a new life, Quentin travels around the country with Grim—sometimes in first-class accommodations—to raise awareness about the millions of strays that are euthanized each year. To decrease the number of dogs without homes, animal welfare advocates like Grim believe in more spaying and neutering centers, the banning of commercial puppy mills, and better education for those who want to ádopt pets.

Nearly 4 million dogs and cats in the United States are put to death in shelters each year. Carbon monoxide gas chambers—a euthanasia method used since World War II—are routinely used in animal shelters throughout the country.

Grim and his colleagues say the method is inhumane. "It's America's dirty little secret," said Grim, who has written the book *Miracle Dog: How Quentin Survived the Gas Chamber to Speak for Animals on Death Row* (Alpine Publishing). "If people actually saw the gas chamber working, they would sign a petition tomorrow to ban it."

At least Quentin got even with the St. Louis gas chamber. Thanks to his and Grim's fund-raising and lobbying efforts, the city's dog pound shut down its gas chamber forever.

A GREAT PYRENEES NAMED ZOE had a close brush
with death—literally. She was swallowed up by a
city street sweeper and survived.

The dog, owned by Gene Fee, of Jefferson
City, Missouri, was out for a walk on a late
November day in 2001. As the street sweeper
approached, the 125-pound white dog unexplain-
ably bolted straight toward the huge machine
and promptly disappeared under it.

John Reutter, who had been driving a truck
behind the sweeper and saw what happened,
immediately called for help. He ordered the oper-
ator of the sweeper to stop. Then Reutter looked
inside the machine and was surprised to see that
Zoe was very much alive and didn't seem too
hurt. But she was stuck between the conveyor
belt and broom about a foot above the ground.

A crew of six city workers, who arrived in
three maintenance vehicles, needed only ten
minutes to remove the bolts, hinges, and broom.
It took another twenty minutes to free the big
dog from an opening they created underneath

the sweeper. Zoe was unhurt but black instead of white.

"She came out and wanted to be petted and reassured," Reutter recalled. "I expected a small dog. But here was this beautiful, white dog, covered with dirt and grease."

An animal control officer who arrived with the city workers found a phone number on Zoe's collar and called her owner who soon was reunited with the dog.

Zoe was taken to a vet who said all she needed after her ordeal were some painkillers and a good shampoo.

DODGER THE BEAGLE had a bear of a time when a mother bruin apparently mistook him for one of her cubs and held him captive in her den.

"It was something I'll never forget, and I suppose the same was true for that beagle dog," owner William "Butch" McCormick, of Wilton, Maine, said in a personal interview.

He and his pooch had gone rabbit hunting on February 6, 1997, deep in the woods. For an unknown reason, Dodger ran off, and even though the dog was wearing a radio collar, McCormick couldn't find him with his handheld receiver. After looking for hours, he reluctantly went home.

Hoping the dog had survived through the bitter subzero night, the hunter returned to the area the next morning and resumed his search for Dodger. "There was about three feet of snow on the ground, so it was hard going," said McCormick. "I thought there was a good chance he was dead or possibly hurt." The dog's collar was still sending a signal so McCormick knew what direction to look.

Two days after Dodger's disappearance, McCormick spotted the dog's tracks and followed them to a snow-covered brush pile that had a hole in it. "The tracks showed he had gone into the hole, so I called to him. I heard him bark and I thought, 'He's still alive!'"

The hunter was overjoyed when Dodger began climbing out from the hole. But the owner's happiness turned to shock when he saw the head of a large black mama bear emerge and gently grab Dodger with its teeth and pull the dog back into her den.

"Dodger got about two-thirds of the way out when a bear grabbed him by the hind legs with its teeth and pulled him back in. I couldn't believe he would be in there with a bear and still be alive. It was startling.

"The bear was a big one. I didn't know how I was going to get the dog out. I knew I needed help."

McCormick went home and returned the following day with Thomas Jacobs, a state game warden. "He didn't believe me at first," said McCormick. "He told me, 'There's no way a beagle is going to be in the den of a bear and still be alive.' But he wanted to see for himself."

They had to snowshoe about two miles back in the woods to reach the den. The warden brought along a shotgun with which he planned to shoot blanks, if necessary, to scare the sow. "I called to Dodger, and we heard him yelping from inside the hole, but he didn't come out because the bear wouldn't let him."

Dodger wasn't the only animal making noises in the den. The men also could hear cubs squealing and whining inside. McCormick and Jacobs left and came back the next day with four wildlife experts, including bear specialist Sandy Ritchie. The team also brought along a jab-stick and a small-caliber rifle, both loaded with tranquilizing darts just in case.

"We couldn't see the dog," Ritchie told reporters later. "We could hear the cubs, and the bear seemed to sense our presence and became more active." She said that hibernating bears could easily be awakened by a disturbance or warm temperatures.

Once again McCormick called the dog, and once again Dodger appeared at the entrance of the den only to be pulled back by the bear. "The dog tried to climb out again, and I kept trying to reach for him," Ritchie said. "She would gently pull him back. It is my opinion that she felt this dog was one of her cubs and was protectively keeping him close to her."

Recalled McCormick, "When Sandy looked into the den, she saw the two cubs underneath the bear's armpits and Dodger was tucked in right next to them. It was unbelievable."

Finally Ritchie was able to grab the dog's collar and pull him out. This allowed the bear to climb out of her den, but when she saw all the humans, she ignored the dog and headed off into the woods.

Looking in the den, the wildlife team spotted two cubs scarcely four weeks old, less than ten inches long and weighing a pound apiece. Fearing the babies would freeze to death without their mother, Ritchie bundled them up in blankets and hoped their mother would return, which she did later that day. However, the next day, she took her cubs and made them a new home in a different den nearby.

As for Dodger, he was dehydrated and hungry, but otherwise fine after his four days of unbearable captivity. "He was yelping and yelping," said McCormick. "I think he was afraid of ending up back in the hole. He was fine by the time we got home. But I never hunted with him after that."

Ironically, even though the bear kidnapped Dodger, she also saved his life. "We could tell he had milk from the bear because you could smell sour milk around his mouth," said McCormick. "He was drinking it just like a cub. She had taken him in and adopted him."

Ritchie said that without the bear's warmth, the beagle probably would not have survived.

In offering a possible explanation for why a bear would mistake a dog for a cub, Ritchie said, "You have to realize that she had her young when she was in a state of semihibernation." Besides, she added, bears apparently can't count very well.

"What is not in doubt is the bear's parenting skills," Ritchie added. "She was very, very gentle with that dog."

A SMALL BLACK TERRIER named Sweetie came back from the grave—literally.

On May 21, 2001, Sweetie was struck by a mail delivery truck in the street in front of her home. When Glenda Stevens, of Park Hills, Missouri, found her dog sprawled on the pavement near the mailbox, she held her pet's limp body and couldn't detect a heartbeat or any breathing.

Convinced that Sweetie was dead, the grief-stricken owner hastily dug a shallow grave in the backyard and buried her beloved pet. Hours later, when Stevens went to show relatives her dog's fresh grave, she saw a sight that shocked her— Sweetie's hind legs were sticking out of the ground, and they were wiggling. The presumed dead dog was not only alive but digging herself out of her grave.

Filled with a swirl of emotions—joy that her dog wasn't dead and guilt for mistakenly burying her pet alive—Stevens rushed Sweetie to the nearest veterinarian who determined that the dog had suffered a broken front leg, a broken jaw, and head injuries. The vet suggested that it would be best to put the animal to sleep. But after seeing Sweetie's will to live, Stevens refused. "She's my baby, and I love her," she told the vet. The dog was stabilized but needed a lot of treatment that Stevens couldn't afford.

Meanwhile, Sweetie's return from the grave made the TV news in nearby St. Louis. After seeing the story, the grooming manager of the Dardenne Animal Medical Center in Wentzville sixty miles away arranged for the practice's owner, veterinarian Mark Lucas, to treat the dog.

"We had to cast the front foot and wire and pin the lower jaw," Dr. Lucas said in a personal interview. The dog remained at the animal hospital for two weeks and recovered relatively quickly. "Then we had to get her on a weight reduction plan because she was so fat," he said.

In fact, the vet added, it was because Sweetie was overweight that she ended up being prematurely buried. "She was so fat that it was hard to tell, even though she was alive, that she was breathing," Dr. Lucas said. "When she was hit, she suffered a head trauma that knocked her unconscious. She was limp and wasn't breathing very deep, so, as traumatized as Glenda was, it would be easy to assume the dog was dead. Fortunately when Glenda buried her, the dog wasn't buried too deep. If Sweetie had been in a six-foot-deep grave, and in her physical condition, she definitely would not have dug herself out."

Sweetie's story was amazing enough to make the news around the world. "After it aired in St. Louis and CNBC, it just snowballed," said Dr. Lucas. "When she went home, there were about twenty cameras. Animal Planet did a piece on her, including a re-creation of her getting buried. A Japanese show came to film the story too. Instead of burying a stuffed animal like Animal Planet did, the Japanese wanted to bury the real dog again. Glenda told them, 'No, go away!'"

A TWO-YEAR-OLD German shepherd–chow mix made it clear that he wasn't going to die before his time.

After being struck by a vehicle on an Arizona highway, the injured pooch lay on the side of the road until two sheriff's deputies arrived. In a bizarre attempt to end the dog's suffering, the deputies choked him and then clubbed him before leaving him for dead all night in the desert.

Unbelievably, the dog survived the car, survived the asphyxiation, survived the bludgeoning, and then survived twelve hours of desert exposure.

About 8:30 p.m. on September 24, 2001, the dog was struck by a hit-and-run driver on a road in Pima, Arizona. The pooch was alive but looked like he was seriously injured. Two deputies from the Pima County Sheriff's Office arrived on the scene and called for a Pima Animal Control officer to take care of him.

After waiting over an hour, the deputies finally decided to put the animal out of his misery because they thought he was suffering and close to death. They contacted their supervisors and were given permission to euthanize the dog as long as they didn't use their guns. Captain Kathleen Brennan later explained that the deputies were not allowed to shoot the animal because of concern over the safety of bystanders. Besides, officials were worried that gunshots at night would unduly alarm area residents.

So the deputies tried to choke the dog. But when that proved unsuccessful, a bystander suggested hitting him between the eyes with a blunt instrument, believing it would bring on a quick death. They took the man's advice. Afterward, the deputies detected no pulse or breathing in the dog and, assuming they had euthanized the animal, left the scene.

The dog remained along the side of the road overnight. The next morning, an animal control officer arrived, thinking he was going to pick up the carcass of a dead dog. Instead he was startled when the canine staggered to his feet and limped underneath the truck. The officer captured the animal and took him to the Southwest Side Veterinary Clinic. The dog suffered bruises, scrapes on the chin, a cut on its left front leg and right front shoulder and a gash on the bridge of the nose where officers struck him. Incredibly, despite all that the animal had been through, he had not suffered permanent head or brain injuries and made a full recovery.

Ironically, Captain Brennan, supervisor of the two deputies involved in the attempted mercy killing, decided to adopt the pooch. She and her family gave him the name Lazarus after the biblical story of Jesus Christ raising his friend, Lazarus, from the dead.

Said Brennan, "After I found out he was still alive, I went, 'Oh, boy. We can't let this dog go through all this and have nobody adopt him and have him put to sleep by Animal Control.' That would be very wrong."

The same word was used by Pima County Sheriff Clarence Dupnik, who made a public apology for the actions of the deputies involved in the case. "We were wrong," Dupnik said in a statement. "I sincerely regret and apologize that this incident occurred, as do the officers involved." No charges were filed against the deputies.

Because of the incident, deputies now receive training in how to deal with injured animals.

LAZARUS WAS ALSO THE NEW NAME given to a seemingly lifeless beagle puppy who was presumed to be roadkill and was about to be cremated. But seconds before being incinerated, he showed a glimmer of life.

Today he's a sweet dog living with a loving adoptive family.

In late January 2004, when he was ten months old, the dog was out roaming when he was struck in the head by a vehicle in a rural area north of Duluth, Georgia. Left for dead by the side of the road, the dog was picked up as roadkill by the sanitation department, stuffed in a body bag, and taken to the Washington-Wilkes Humane Animal Shelter for incineration.

Just before the dog was set for cremation, shelter director Gloria Wheatley checked to see if the animal matched the description of any missing pets. She was stunned when she realized the dog was alive—but barely breathing. "I shut the bag real quick because I didn't believe what I was seeing," Wheatley told the Associated Press. "In fourteen years [of handling dead animals], it's the first time this has ever happened, believe you me."

The cold, unresponsive, comatose beagle was taken to a veterinarian. Even though the vet gave the pup little chance of surviving through the night, veterinary technician Becki Walker volunteered to provide care for him. Walker stayed by his side throughout the next day, monitoring his condition, holding him, and feeding him with a syringe.

After two days, Lazarus was still in a coma, but his brain showed signs of activity. The dog's back legs, which had been paralyzed, began to move. The following day, the pup was on his feet but suffered motor skill problems from a brain injury. That's when Walker gave the dog the Bible-inspired name Lazarus. "This is a unique situation of an animal that had enough heart and guts to keep going every day," she said.

The owner of the beagle didn't want to be responsible for the medical bills so custody was given to the Companion Animal Rescue League, which paid the tab.

Two weeks after the accident, Lazarus was released from the animal hospital and given to beagle lover Linda Blauch, of Duluth, then president of the league, to foster until he was well enough to be adopted. "When he first arrived at home, Lazarus wasn't all together there neurologically," she said in a personal interview. "He would get panic attacks and get nervous very easily. He tended to walk around in circles to the right and he had a dazed look in his eyes. He also yawned a lot and constantly stuck out his tongue.

"He eventually began interacting with me and my other dogs and acted more like a normal beagle. But the vet said Lazarus will never be perfectly right because of his severe head injury."

After the story of the dog's close encounter with death made the national wires, Blauch received calls from all over the country, and even Canada, wanting to adopt him. However, she eventually adopted out Lazarus to a local family. "He's now a very lovable, sweet dog," she said. "I still dog-sit for him when they go out of town.

"A lot of times when we adopt out a dog, the people change its name. But we all knew that Lazarus' name would stay the same because it's perfect for him."

WHEN FLOSSY THE DOG disappeared and didn't return during a walk with his owners, they had given up hope of ever seeing him again.

They didn't know that the seven-year-old Icelandic shepherd had fallen into the bottom of a dried-out well and couldn't get out. Amazingly, he survived for more than two months without food until he was discovered and returned to his stunned and happy owners.

The shepherd had been walking without a leash with his owners Birgitte Pontoppidan and her husband in the countryside near Copenhagen, Denmark, in June 2003. Suddenly, the dog took off to chase a rabbit, but didn't return.

His heartbroken owners put up posters and handed out flyers, hoping to find their lost dog, but they heard nothing. "After a month we had to realize he was gone," Birgitte told reporters. "We figured he had been run over by a car and had crept under a bush and died."

They were so convinced that Flossy was dead that they bought a new pet to replace him.

But Flossy hadn't died. While chasing the rabbit, the dog had fallen twelve feet down an old well that had been covered by bushes. He might have died there if a passerby hadn't heard whimpering coming from the bottom of the pit. When the man went to investigate, he was shocked to discover the trapped dog. He got Flossy out and, with the help of the dog's tags, contacted the owners who were thrilled with the unexpected news.

More than two months without food had left Flossy extremely weak. His weight had dropped by nearly half from his original fifty pounds. Another week in the well, and it's likely he would have died, Birgitte said. The dog had survived by drinking rainwater.

"It's incredible to have him back," she declared. "Our veterinarian said it's close to impossible for a dog to survive so long without food." To help Flossy gain back his weight, she served him all his favorite foods.

WHEN BENSON THE BOXER dashed to the edge of a 400-foot seaside cliff and disappeared, his grief-stricken owner Martin Greenwood was convinced he was dead. A search failed to find the dog's body.

So you can imagine how shocked Greenwood was when he learned that his "dead" dog turned up eight days later—injured but very much alive—at a pub two miles from the scene of the accident.

"It's a miracle," declared Greenwood. "He must be the toughest and luckiest dog in the world. I couldn't believe it when they told me he was alive."

On an April day in 2004, Greenwood was taking pictures when the boxer plunged off the cliff near Contisbury Hill, North Devon, England. "I saw Benson sprint off toward the cliff edge at great speed," Greenwood told the London *Sun*. "I shouted to him, then tried to chase after him but when I got to the edge, he'd gone." Because the tide had come in, Greenwood assumed that the dog had hit the water and drowned. If the tide had been out, he reasoned, Benson's body would have been spotted on the rocky beach.

"I alerted the Coast Guard, the police, and all the locals," he recalled. "We scoured the cliffs but there was no sign of him. I kept imagining his body floating in the water and just hoped he had a quick death."

Greenwood later checked tide times so he could look for Benson's body on the beach when the tide was out.

Eight days later, while Benson's owner was still mourning the loss of his four-year-old dog, patrons and employees at the Exmoor Sandpiper Inn in Lynton, Devon, were amused when a boxer showed up at their doorstep. Louise Herbst, the pub's landlady, told the paper, "He had a few cuts and bruises but we cleaned him up and he was fine. He sat with us in the bar. We all fell in love with him. He is such a lovely dog and we would have liked to have kept him."

But they figured he was probably lost and called the animal warden who discovered

Benson's microchip, which made it easy to track down the dog's owner. The warden phoned Greenwood at his home in Porlock, Somerset, with the news.

"When the dog warden said they'd found him, I thought they meant his body," Greenwood recalled. "But they said he was safe and well, and I was over the moon."

When he was reunited with his dog, Greenwood gave Benson a swig of beer.

Interestingly, Benson received an award from the Royal Humane Society two years earlier. The dog had spotted a woman attempting suicide in the North Tyne River, Northumbria, and alerted Martin by barking. Martin called police and the woman was saved.

A FOUR-MONTH-OLD BLACK LAB MIX proved to be one hard-headed puppy. He had a head-on collision with a freight train—and survived.

While driving in his car on January 3, 2002, Dana Oliver, of Eugene, Oregon, pulled up to a railroad crossing in nearby Junction City and spotted the puppy and another dog playing near the tracks. When a train approached at about 25 mph, the older dog moved out of the way. But the puppy panicked.

"The little dog got spooked," Oliver told the Eugene *Register-Guard*. "It was trying to look for a space between the cars to slip through, and it jumped up and then the corner of a boxcar hit it in the head. As soon as the train passed, I scooped the puppy up. I thought he died in my arms. He was whimpering, and then he stopped and let loose of his bowels."

The pup was still alive, so Oliver rushed the limp, unconscious dog to Whitlock's Countryside Animal Clinic. Veterinarian Mary Whitlock quickly assessed the male dog. He was bleeding from his nose and had a big lump over his right eye, but had no obvious fractures and had good withdrawal reflexes in all four legs. She decided to treat him, even though the dog had no collar or identification tag and his owner was unknown. The dog was underfed and had worms and fleas.

"Euthanasia was a real option, too," said Whitlock, who decided to take a chance because of the puppy's age and potential to be placed in a good home.

The dog received intravenous fluids, along with injections of cortisone, antibiotics, and pain medication. By the next afternoon, the puppy regained consciousness and began taking a few steps. "He was very hungry when he started coming around at about two o'clock," Whitlock said. "He wanted to go outside at four o'clock, and by ten o'clock, he had a tail wag and was giving kisses."

After suffering a severe concussion, the puppy amazed the vet with his incredibly fast recovery. "I don't know why this dog's alive," Whitlock said as the puppy wandered around an examination room, pestering her for treats.

The staff at the animal clinic decided to give him an appropriate name. They called him Bonk.

The pup was turned over to the Lane County Animal Regulation Authority's shelter where officers found his owners, transients who couldn't afford his care. The shelter then took full custody of Bonk and found him a loving adoptive home—but not before some controversy.

Recalled a senior animal welfare officer, "Through a misunderstanding, CNN Headline News carried a crawl at the bottom of its telecast saying something like 'Eugene, Oregon, puppy that survived hit by train now faces euthanasia.' For the next day, we fielded irate phone calls from all over the country—even overseas—demanding that Bonk be saved. We weren't going to euthanize him, not after what he went through."

A DOG THAT HAD BEEN TRAPPED in a badger hole for seventeen days finally managed to escape and make her way home. What made her survival even more remarkable was that she couldn't eat throughout her ordeal because she was muzzled.

But then again, maybe that's what saved her life. You see, Sadie was terribly overweight. By not eating, she eventually lost enough weight to wriggle out of the hole.

The fifteen-month-old Patterdale terrier was out walking with her owner's children on a moor in May 2005 near Penzance in Cornwall, England, when she disappeared down a badger set and failed to reappear. (Badgers live in families in a maze of underground tunnels and chambers called a set.) Sadie apparently got stuck.

After a frantic search by RSPCA Inspector Paul Kempson and Sadie's owner, Karen Paynter, of Trewellard, the rescue had to be abandoned. "The badger set was large, with around fifteen entrance holes," Kempson told *K-9* magazine. "We couldn't hear any noise despite constantly calling out her name, and the area around the set was overgrown with bramble and gorse bushes. It was a real effort but eventually we had to give up.

"Rescuing dogs that become trapped underground can be very difficult and dangerous not only for the dog but also for our inspectors. Dealing with a distressed pet at the same time and possibly a badger creates quite a challenge."

Badger sets are protected by law, so the RSPCA would have needed to apply for a special license to dig out a pet. "We continued to visit the site each day, but became increasingly concerned because the dog had a muzzle on and would be unable to feed," said the inspector.

When two weeks passed, Paynter was convinced that her dog was dead. "The RSPCA man said he had had a case where a dog survived eleven days down a hole, so after that time I thought that was it."

But then on June 16 at 5 a.m.—seventeen days after Sadie went missing—Paynter was awakened by a whimpering noise outside her door. To her happy surprise, there stood a dirty and extremely skinny Sadie. The dog had lost so much weight that her head looked larger than her body. She was covered in fleas and ticks, but otherwise was OK.

Paynter said she was "over the moon" to have Sadie back, and joked that the enforced diet while in the badger's set had been good for her overweight dog.

After a thorough veterinary examination, Sadie was given the all clear to go home, where she immediately went to sleep.

"This is a remarkable story of survival considering Sadie was trapped underground for such a long period and wearing a muzzle," said RSPCA Chief Inspector Les Sutton. "Yet she was able to survive and extricate herself from such a predicament.

"Usually dogs in these circumstances manage to get themselves free after four to six days. Sadie is a very lucky dog."

A STRAY HOUND was accidentally imprisoned for three weeks without food or water under the floor of a building under construction.

Not until a night security guard at the Jasmine Park senior-center construction site in Grants Pass, Oregon, spotted the dog's eyes through a crack in the newly built floor did anybody realize that the dog had been trapped. On July 5, 2003, security guard Lance Lyndh called the city Department of Public Safety to report the confined female hound. Police arrived and cut a hole in the floor and allowed two men to coax the dog out with a bowl of water.

"She's a miracle dog," said Chris Nelson, thirty-two, one of the two rescuers. "It was about the size of a dalmatian, if it had been filled out, and it was scared."

Nelson wrapped the dog in a sheet and placed her in a construction shed until police took her to the vet. The hound got her first comfortable night's sleep in weeks at the Pacific Veterinary Clinic, where she remained until a permanent home was found for her.

The construction site was a forty-three-bed senior center that was replacing a building that had burned down four months earlier. Crews nailed the final floorboard down on June 16, said Bill Thatcher, the construction superintendent. Workers never knew that the stray dog was underneath because they never saw or heard her, he said.

"For a dog to survive that long without food or drink is amazing," Thatcher said.

The hound was given the name Phoenix because she rose from the ashes of the burned senior center.

CAP, A BORDER COLLIE who had been given up for dead, was found alive after surviving for two months trapped in a hole on a freezing cliff. Ironically, he was discovered by another border collie who was in training as a mountain rescue dog.

"He is a miracle dog to our family," said his owner Jo Walker.

The eight-year-old pet was on a walk with Jo and her husband the Reverend Gavin Walker on October 28, 2001, at St. Bees Head, Cumbria, England. The dog took off running because he was afraid of the fireworks that someone had set off nearby. "We last saw him running toward the sea," Jo recalled. They assumed he had fallen off the cliff. "The tide was heavy so we thought we'd never see him again."

The reverend and his wife, who lived in nearby Egremont, had scoured the area for hours after Cap went missing. They had even spent the night near the spot where they had lost him and searched for him for several more days, all to no avail. Eventually they came to the belief that their beloved dog had perished.

But he hadn't. Cap had fallen down a five-foot-deep rocky hole on the edge of the cliff and become trapped. For the next eight weeks, as the weather turned colder and nastier, the dog managed to survive on rainwater and a few dandelions.

He certainly would have died if it hadn't been for a fellow border collie named Rosie, owned by Stephen and Saffron Price-Walter.

The couple, from Eskdale, had just started training Rosie as a search and rescue dog. While out for a walk on Christmas Day, she came to a hole on the crumbling cliffs at St. Bees Head and started barking excitedly until her owners joined her. They looked down the hole and spotted a skeletal, nearly comatose border collie lying on the bottom. It was Cap.

"He was very thin and shell-shocked," Saffron recalled. "The weather here was getting colder and frostier every evening, so I don't think he would have survived much longer."

Stephen climbed into the hole and lifted out the bedraggled dog. Because Cap still had his collar and tags, it was easy for the couple to contact the owners with the amazing news. "When we telephoned his owners, we couldn't believe how long he'd been surviving out there," Saffron said.

The Walkers, who rejoiced over the news that Cap was alive, were even more incredulous. "It was a Christmas miracle," Jo gushed.

Cap lost about half his body weight, but he soon recovered. The Walkers had adopted Cap from a farm because he was unsuitable to herd sheep. "Border collies have an obsession with running off," said Jo. "But hopefully with all the love and attention he's getting from us and the other villagers, we won't lose him again."

FRANK THE CHIHUAHUA survived an attack by a cougar that had carted him off for a late-night snack.

On June 24, 2001, Frank and his much larger canine companion Bear were chasing rabbits in Terry Herberts' backyard in Port Alberni, British Columbia. About 9:30 p.m., a wild cougar leaped into the yard, snapped up Frank, and darted off into the bushes with its prey.

According to the *Alberni Valley Times*, Herberts and her children heard the dog yelp, and arrived only in time to see the tiny dog's limp body being carried off into the woods in the big cat's mouth. Bear bravely gave chase, but he was unable to keep up with the swift and cunning predator.

The distraught family contacted a local hunter who told them a cougar often buries its prey and then returns later, sometimes in two or three days, to devour its catch.

Meanwhile, Bear headed out in search of his little buddy early the next morning with family members following behind him. Soon Bear's ears perked up, and he started whining. The family began to call for Frank, and to their joy they began to hear a faint reply. Twenty minutes later they found Frank under some brush, wounded but alive. Although he was severely bruised with several internal injuries, remarkably there were no bite marks, nor any life-threatening lesions common to most cougar attacks.

"Cougar teeth usually leave pretty good holes that would snap something like a Chihuahua in half," Dr. Hugo Lambrechts, Frank's veterinarian, told the paper. Conservation officer Ralph Escott added, "They kill with the initial attack. Bite it, snap it, and incapacitate it. They usually consume part of it right away and then bury it."

It's believed Frank survived by playing dead and the cougar gave him a premature burial. But then again, maybe the big cat was looking for a bigger meal. "In the case of a Chihuahua, there isn't much there to eat," Escott said.

Defenders

Buster, a five-year-old springer spaniel, did what British troops had failed to do—uncover a cache of weapons and explosives hidden by an armed resistance cell in the southern Iraqi town of Safwan.

In March 2003, the bomb-sniffing member of the Royal Army Veterinary Corps was ordered to Safwan after troops suspected a building was the headquarters of extremists responsible for vicious attacks on British soldiers. An initial raid of the site by 200 troops failed to turn up any weapons.

"The soldiers had found nothing so I unleashed Buster and sent him in," the dog's handler, Sgt. Danny Morgan, later told embedded correspondents. "The rule is that the dog always goes first in case there are booby traps, and I was obviously concerned for him as he started his search. Within minutes he became excited in a particular area, and I knew he'd discovered something."

The springer spaniel had stopped and stared at a wardrobe. When Morgan and other soldiers went to investigate, they realized Buster had found a cache of arms—even though the enemy had hidden it in a wall cavity, covered it with a sheet of tin, then pushed a wardrobe in front to conceal everything. Inside the secret hideaway were Russian AK47 assault rifles, a pistol, six grenades, fuses, ammunition, suitcases full of large quantities of cash, two kilograms of cocaine, and pro-Saddam literature.

"We would never have found the weapons without him, and they would still be a threat to our troops and the local population," Morgan said.

The springer spaniel's find led to the arrest of sixteen Saddam Hussein supporters and defused a violent cell of insurgents. There were no attacks in the town since Buster's discovery, and soon afterward troops were able to replace their steel helmets with soft berets.

Because of his accomplishment, Buster became the twenty-fourth dog to receive the Dickin Medal—the highest decoration for gallantry that can be bestowed on any animal member of the British and Commonwealth forces. He was given the medal in a ceremony in England in December 2003.

Morgan, who was based at the military dogs' training school in southern England, said it was "fantastic" for Buster to be recognized for succeeding where humans had failed. "I'm very proud of him."

Before the war, the springer spaniel had been the family pet of Sgt. Morgan, his wife Nicki, and their daughter Emma in their home in Aldershot, Hants, England. Morgan trained Buster by teaching him to fetch weapons like guns and ammunition instead of sticks and balls.

But then the sergeant and his dog were deployed to Iraq. Buster was so valuable to the army that he was even given his own protective gear in case of chemical or biological attack. When a Scud missile or gas attack warning sounded, he leaped into a special sealed pen equipped with an electric motor that pumped air through a gas mask filter.

"He loves his job simply because he thinks it's a game, and obviously has no idea he's going into dangerous situations," Morgan told reporters in 2003. "I end up doing all the worrying because he's not only doing a job out here—he's my best friend."

OF THE ESTIMATED 4,000 American war dogs that served in Vietnam, Nemo was perhaps the most famous because of the incredible valor he showed during an attack.

Despite being shot in the head, the German shepherd charged enemy guns, knocked down two Viet Cong, and then crawled back to his wounded master and shielded him from bullets during a fierce firefight. In 1964, when Nemo was eighteen months old, he began training as an air force sentry dog, and in January 1966 was assigned to the 377th Security Police Squadron, stationed at Tan Son Nhut Air Base in South Vietnam. He was eventually paired with a new handler, Airman 2nd Class Robert Thorneburg, twenty-two.

In the early morning hours of December 4, 1966, the base was attacked by sixty Viet Cong. The Americans repelled the assault although three airmen and their dogs had died in the fighting. By daybreak, the search patrols believed that all the infiltrators had been killed or captured. The Americans were wrong.

The next night, Thorneburg and Nemo were assigned duty near an old Vietnamese graveyard about a quarter mile from the air base's runways. Shortly after the soldier and his dog started their patrol, several Viet Cong opened fire. Thorneburg released his canine and together they charged the enemy. But within seconds, Nemo was felled when he took a bullet that entered under his right eye and exited through his mouth. Meanwhile, Thorneburg killed one Viet Cong before he was shot in the shoulder and knocked to the ground.

Despite the severe pain from his head wound, the black and tan eighty-five-pound dog picked himself up and attacked the guerrillas, buying Thorneburg just enough time to radio for backup forces. When a Quick Reaction Team arrived, Nemo crawled over to his master and covered him with his body as bullets whizzed by in a deadly firefight. Nemo stayed with Thorneburg until the Americans had killed the remaining eight Viet Cong.

Even after help arrived, the dog wouldn't allow anyone to touch his master for several minutes, but soon he relented and both were taken back to the base for medical attention. Thorneburg had to be evacuated to a hospital in Japan to recuperate, so the handler tearfully said goodbye to the dog who had saved his life. The airman eventually recovered from his wounds and returned home with honors.

Lt. Raymond T. Hutson, the base vet, managed to save Nemo's life although the dog was left blind in one eye. After several skin grafts, Nemo was put back on perimeter duty, but his wounds needed further treatment. Six months after the attack, the air force ordered Nemo returned to the United States with honors—the first sentry dog in the Vietnam War to be officially retired from active service.

On July 22, 1967, Nemo arrived at Kelly Air Force Base, Texas, where Captain Robert M. Sullivan, the officer in charge of the sentry dog training program, welcomed him home. "I have to keep from getting involved with individual dogs in this program," Sullivan said at the time, "but I can't help feeling a little emotional about this dog. He shows how valuable a dog is to his handler in staying alive."

Nemo and Captain Sullivan made several cross-country tours and television appearances as part of the air force's recruitment drive for more war dog candidates. Nemo then spent the rest of his retirement at the Department of Defense Dog

Center at Lackland Air Force Base, Texas. Near the veterinary facility, the canine was given a permanent kennel that had a sign with his name, serial number, and details of his Vietnam heroic exploits. Nemo died in December 1972 at the age of ten.

According to the Vietnam Dog Handler Association, more than 4,000 dogs served in that conflict in more than 88,000 army missions in which at least 3,800 enemy soldiers were killed and 1,200 captured.

"Without them, there would have been another 10,000 names on the [Vietnam Veterans Memorial] Wall," Ron Aiello told the Scripps Howard News Service. Aiello said he had walked point on patrol in Vietnam for thirteen months with his beloved Stormy, who saved his life and those of other GIs "more times than I could count."

Sadly, only an extremely small number of these loyal canines ever returned to the United States. Because the Pentagon considered the dogs "surplus equipment," the dogs were either euthanized by the U.S. military, turned over to the South Vietnamese Army, or simply abandoned as America hustled to pull out of the unpopular conflict. It's estimated that 3,000 war dogs died during the Vietnam War.

Former Vietnam War dog handler John Burnam, who has lobbied Congress to authorize a memorial for the brave animals said, "These dogs knew more of honor, devotion, and duty than most people today."

DURING THE INVASION OF SICILY in World War II, a mixed breed named Chips captured—by himself—six enemy soldiers who tried to ambush an American patrol.

It was quite a remarkable feat for a dog that had once been a sweet family pet.

Within months after Pearl Harbor was attacked, the American Kennel Club and a new group calling itself Dogs for Defense mobilized dog owners across the country to donate their pets. Chips, then four years old, was one of the first to join the War Dog Program. He had been the family pet of the Edward Wren family of Pleasantville, New York, until they turned him over to the U.S. Army for combat training. More than 10,000 donated dogs were trained for sentry duty, scouting and patrolling, mine detection and delivering messages, according to the archives of the U.S. Army Quartermaster Museum in Fort Lee, Virginia.

Chips, the son of a part-shepherd, part-collie father and a northern sled-dog mother, and his handler, Private John P. Rowell, were assigned to the 3rd Infantry Division, 30th Infantry Regiment. They served with that unit in North Africa, Sicily, Italy, France, and Germany. An affectionate canine who had a particularly keen sense of smell and hearing, Chips proved to be a good soldier and was popular with the troops—especially after saving their lives.

When American forces invaded Sicily in July 1943, Chips waded ashore with his handler and his platoon. Once they had established a

beachhead 300 yards inland, the soldiers reached
an abandoned pillbox and took a short rest. But
Chips sensed danger nearby and—going counter
to what he had been trained—he broke away from
his handler and dashed toward a camouflaged
machine-gun nest. It erupted in gunfire. Although
a bullet grazed his head, Chips ignored the pain
and leaped into the nest. The firing ceased and
was followed by deadly silence. When his squad
arrived, they saw Chips holding onto the throat
of the enemy gunner, and five other terrified men
with their arms raised in surrender.

After being treated for a scalp wound and
powder burns, the dog returned to duty that same
night. Within a couple of hours, Chips alerted
his troops that an enemy squad was sneaking up
behind them. Private Rowell and his comrades
then quickly captured ten Italian soldiers and
held them as prisoners.

Determined to honor Chips, Lt. Lucian
Truscott recommended the Silver Star and
Purple Heart for the dog, citing how "his coura-
geous action in single-handedly eliminating a

dangerous machine-gun nest and causing the surrender of its crew had prevented injury and death to his men." But the army brass denied the medals request, saying those honors were for human soldiers only. So Chips' friends presented him with a special ribbon with an arrowhead for the assault landing at Sicily and a battle star for each of the eight campaigns in which the dog served.

During the war, Chips also acted as a sentry for President Franklin Roosevelt and British Prime Minister Winston Churchill at their historic conference in Casablanca in 1943. (According to some unconfirmed reports, Chips showed a complete lack of respect for rank and nipped at General Dwight Eisenhower.)

When the war ended, Chips, like many combat dogs, was sent back to the United States to a reprocessing section for rehabilitation to civilian life. As reporters and photographers recorded his return home in 1945, the Wrens and their three children hugged him. "He doesn't seem to wag his tail as much as before going to war," Ed Wren told reporters at the time, "but I suppose he is suffering from battle fatigue."

A photograph taken shortly after Chips' return showed him happily pulling four-year-old Johnny Wren through the snow on a sled. But the dog's happiness was short-lived. Seven months after coming home, he died from complications from war injuries. He was buried at the Hartsdale Pet Cemetery in New York.

MIQUETTE THE FOX TERRIER was used to war. Ever since she was a puppy, she had seen countless battles while sticking close to her master, French soldier Andre Fournier. So when the dog found Fournier and his fellow troops in a life-and-death situation, she knew exactly what to do to help save them.

Miquette and her master had enlisted in the French Army when World War I began. During battle marches, she rode on the back of Fournier's knapsack and crouched by his side during combat. Whenever the troops had settled into their trenches, she strolled back and forth, wagging her tail, to keep their spirits up.

In a fierce battle against German soldiers near Arras, France, in December 1914, a shell exploded in the trench where Fournier and his platoon were fighting. Everyone was buried under the debris except Miquette. The little dog scratched and sniffed on top of the rubble but was unable to reach any of the men.

Knowing they needed help, Miquette scampered toward the next trench. Although deadly bullets whizzed by her, she made it safely. Then she whined and ran back and forth in the trench until some of the soldiers realized she was trying to tell them something. She climbed out of their trench and led them to the caved-in trench. They pulled out all the victims, including Fournier, who had suffered several broken ribs. All were still alive. They had survived thanks to the quick-thinking combat canine Miquette.

TALK ABOUT A DOGGED PURSUIT.

Kaiser the police dog was chasing several muggers when he was struck by a car. He got back on his feet and caught up to one of the crooks only to be beaten by passersby who thought he was a mad dog. Despite it all, the canine cop got his man.

The German shepherd was on patrol in Brockley, England, on April 21, 2004, when officers spotted four teenage robbers speeding off on their mountain bikes. Kaiser ran after them and was ready to pounce on one of the crooks when he was accidentally hit by a car.

Fortunately, he took only a glancing blow that momentarily stunned him. When he gathered his wits, the dog shook off the pain of the impact and got back on his feet and continued the chase.

He finally managed to catch up to one of the cyclists and pulled the suspect off the bike by biting into his right arm. That should have been the end of it, but it wasn't. Kaiser had the bad luck of nabbing the suspect in front of two passersby who assumed the police dog was a crazed dog because the young man was screaming for help.

Unaware Kaiser was performing his police duty, they began beating him with a baseball bat and a metal vacuum cleaner pipe. Despite the pounding, Kaiser bravely held his grip on the arm of the yelling suspect. But after a painful blow to the back of his head from the vacuum cleaner pipe, the dog let go of the youth.

Before the thief could flee, however, Terry West, Kaiser's handler and police constable, arrived and arrested the suspect on suspicion of attempted robbery. The youth was driven by ambulance to Lewisham Hospital with six puncture wounds on his right elbow. Although bruised and battered, Kaiser was not seriously injured.

The two-year-old dog was honored for his dedication and perseverance at a police commendations ceremony. "Kaiser had been out of dog school for only four months," West told reporters. "What's so special is he was a young dog, and to prove his bravery in such circumstances is highly commendable. The dog put his life on the line to do his job. I'm extremely proud of him."

A 116-POUND Rhodesian ridgeback named Rocky thwarted the attempted kidnapping of an eight-year-old girl by a convicted sex offender.

On the night of August 30, 1998, Mike and Joan Staples and their daughter Laura had just gone to sleep on the second floor of their three-story house in Hatboro, Pennsylvania. A short while later, an intruder quietly broke into their home and crept up the stairs to Laura's room. He clamped his hand over the girl's mouth to muffle her screams and lifted her off the bed. All the struggling girl could do in the midst of her horror was to kick her bedroom door with her bare foot as the intruder carried her out of her room and down the stairs.

The thud from Laura's kick on the door woke up Rocky, who was sleeping on the third floor, and alerted him that something was wrong. The dog charged down two flights of stairs. Seeing a strange man clutching the terror-stricken girl, Rocky bared his teeth and threw his massive body against the intruder. The man dropped

Laura and dashed out the door, but Rocky chased
after him and bit him numerous times.

The dog's love and concern for Laura was
stronger than his desire to continue chasing the
assailant, so Rocky let him flee into the dark.
The dog ran back to the house to check on
Laura, who was now sobbing in the arms of her
parents.

They called the police, who soon found the
would-be kidnapper hiding in a nearby park.
The man, who was bleeding from several dog
bites, was arrested and later convicted on
several counts, including assault and attempted
kidnapping.

For his swift and heroic actions, Rocky was
honored in 2000 with the National Hero Dog
Award by the Society for the Prevention of
Cruelty to Animals in Los Angeles. "This act of
protection by the family dog is directly related to
the fact that the dog is loved and cared for by his
family," said the society's chapter president,
Madeline Bernstein. "His act to protect a
member of his pack is instinctual; protecting

Laura was instinctual because he is a true member of the Staples pack."

Laura's mother Joan said, "Rocky has spared our family an unspeakable horror. There's no way we can overstate our gratitude for his bravery and quick response."

CASPER THE SHIH TZU was just a small light-weight furball, but he proved to be a giant in bringing a violent man to justice.

The little lapdog not only helped prevent a brutal rape, he also made legal history by providing incontestable evidence in court that resulted in the conviction of the assailant.

According to court records, about 4 a.m. on September 22, 2000, a sixty-year-old woman was sleeping soundly in her second-floor apartment in Simi Valley, California, when her dog Casper began barking furiously. Awakened by her shih tzu, the woman saw a man, who had entered through an open sliding door, standing in the doorway of her bedroom. She threw a jewelry box at him, grabbed the phone, and tried to call 911. But the intruder knocked the phone out of her hand, struck her in the face, and tried to rape her.

While the woman fought the attacker, Casper leaped on the bed and bit and scratched him. Eventually, the woman escaped his grasp long enough to dial 911 and report the assault. When she told her attacker that the police were on their way, he fled the scene—but not before Casper had left incriminating evidence on him.

After the police arrived, the woman identified her assailant as Soum Laykham, twenty-four, her next-door neighbor. Simi Valley investigators arrested Laykham, who matched the woman's description—even to the tattoo on his left forearm. He also had what looked like claw marks from a dog. However, he denied the charges, leaving Simi Valley police without much substantial evidence.

Then detectives remembered that there was a second witness present at the scene—Casper.

They returned to the suspect's home and took samples of dog hairs found on his pants.

Forensic experts were able to match Casper's DNA to hairs that were found on Laykham's pants. Known as genetic fingerprinting, DNA matching has been widely accepted as conclusive evidence in court cases since the early 1990s. But pet DNA had never been used as evidence in California, and in fact, up until that time, had been admitted in court only once before, in the state of Washington in 1998. In that case, two men were accused of killing a couple and their dog. The dog's blood was found on the clothes of the accused and helped convict them of the double homicide.

Although courts had been reluctant to accept dog DNA, Judge Kevin J. McGee, presiding over Laykham's trial, heard testimony from experts that a canine's DNA was as reliable as a human's. Judge McGee ruled that the procedures for testing canine DNA were not new and are generally the same as those used for testing human DNA.

According to court testimony, Casper's hairs were sent to Joy Halverson, a scientist in Davis, California, who had conducted the DNA testing in the Washington murder case. Halverson, who did DNA testing for the American Kennel Club, had a genetic database of about 470 dogs of different breeds. Using the database, a statistician found that the odds of certainty were 230 million to one that the dog hair on Laykham's pants belonged to Casper.

In the landmark California case, a jury in 2002 found Laykham guilty of residential burglary and assault with intent to commit rape. He was sentenced to six years in state prison.

Casper's hair "was really, really great evidence," Senior Deputy District Attorney Lisa Lee told reporters after the verdict. "I think it was a very important part of the case. We talked to the jury after the verdict and they found it to be very interesting and good science."

Lee praised the brave shih tzu for all that the little dog had done, declaring, "Not only did

Casper bark and save her from being raped, but Casper was key in getting this guy convicted."

Cookie, a German shepherd mix, was a timid, shy dog. And although he enjoyed taking walks in New York's Central Park with his mistress, he tended to cower around other people. In fact, he acted like a sissy dog, especially because he wore booties.

But when his owner was brutally attacked by a ferocious would-be rapist, Cookie turned into a raging guard dog and helped drive off the knife-wielding assailant.

"My dog saved my life," declared Carina Schlesinger, twenty-five, a former European fashion model who had adopted the sixty-pound brown and black dog when he was a puppy four years earlier from a New Jersey animal shelter. "Before this happened, people in the park would ask me about what Cookie would do to protect me because he's such a scaredy-cat," she said. "I would always say Cookie would run away."

But when it counted most, her dog showed just how brave and loyal he was.

As she did every morning at around 8:30, Schlesinger was walking Cookie in the park on that unforgettable day in May 2004. The area normally is filled with other people walking their dogs or jogging along the path, but on this morning, the area was empty. A man in his twenties approached Schlesinger and tried to strike up a conversation with her, asking her questions about the doggie boots Cookie was wearing. She told him it was because the dog had allergies.

Schlesinger then kept walking with Cookie, but when the man appeared on the path again minutes later, she demanded to know if he was following her. Suddenly he pounced on her and began choking and punching her and tried to rape her. "He said he had a knife, and he just kept saying, 'I'm gonna kill you . . . I'm gonna cut you,'" she recalled.

But the woman, who had taken karate and kickboxing classes, fought back. Seeing his mistress in danger, Cookie sprang into action and leaped on the attacker. He wound up biting him three times. "When it came down to it, Cookie turned into a Braveheart and did something he would have never done before," Schlesinger said.

The dog and his mistress proved too much for the attacker, and he ran off.

But police were able to collect samples of the assailant's blood—caused by Cookie's bites—that were on the victim's clothes. DNA analysis revealed the identity of the attacker—a career criminal named Tito Rodriguez, thirty-three. Eventually, police arrested the suspect and brought him to trial. He was later convicted on all counts.

As for Cookie, Schlesinger said, "He's still a coward. But the instinct that came [during the attack] was amazing. I'm very proud of him." She said that if her dog could talk, he would tell the attacker, "I'll bite you again."

HUBERT THE BOUVIER was an imposing dog— large and black with a beard and bushy eyebrows that drooped down over his eyes. But beneath it all, Hubert was a pussycat.

Every day he accompanied his owner Nancy Theis to her job as a hotel manager in Mount Holly, New Jersey. Hubert loved to greet guests and visit people on the streets in town. Because of his gentle, friendly nature, Theis figured that he had been shortchanged on protection instincts, which are usually strong in his breed. She was certain that with his happy, friendly nature, Hubert would be no help if she were in danger.

She learned otherwise on New Year's Day, 1990.

Theis and Hubert had gone out for their regular early morning run around the schoolyard. The stars were still out, and it was dark and cold. As they started heading through a clump of trees, Hubert inexplicably jumped in front of Theis and turned sideways, blocking her path. He wouldn't let her take another step.

"I said, 'What's with you?'" Theis recalled in a personal interview. "But Hubert would not budge. He kept staring at a nearby shed along the route. I kept saying, 'Come on, Hubert, let's go.' But each time I tried to move around him, he took his position, blocking me." Three times she tried to get him to move with no success.

Suddenly, a man jumped out of the darkness from the roof of the shed right in front of them. He was wild-eyed and dirty, as if he had spent the night hiding in the bushes. The man stopped and glared at Theis.

Hubert, standing between them, stared him down. From deep in the dog's throat came a low, menacing growl. Theis had never before heard such a sound coming from her usually friendly pet.

Seconds later, the man bolted. Theis wanted to hurry in the other direction, but the dog refused to move. Hubert stood like a statue for several minutes, his eyes locked on the unsavory character, and wouldn't turn away until he was sure the man was out of sight.

Less than an hour later, Theis was in her kitchen making breakfast and listening to the radio when she heard a local news report that gave her the creeps. Across the schoolyard, not far from where she and Hubert had been walking, two people had been murdered during the night, and police were hunting for the killer.

She immediately phoned police to tell them about her encounter. "The officer told me that they had just caught the suspect," she recalled. "It wasn't far from the spot where Hubert's growl had sent the stranger fleeing."

Police believe that after the double homicide, the man hid in the shed until Theis and Hubert unwittingly flushed him out.

"Hubert had never shown any sign of protective behavior before, but from that point on, I had no doubts about him," Theis said. "The instincts are in there. If trouble came in the front door, he'd know just what to do."

TWICE IN THE SPAN OF THREE MONTHS, Kaiser the German shepherd came to the rescue of people in serious danger.

The dog spent his days in the New York candy store of his master, Angelo Fiocchi. One June night in 1926, Kaiser was sleeping in the back room when he heard some noise in the store. The dog pushed open the door and saw that his master had been cornered by two masked men who threatened to hurt him if he didn't give them all his money.

With a growl, Kaiser sprang into action. He charged into the store and chased the assailants out into the street. He let them get away only because he ran back to make sure that his master was all right. Fortunately, Fiocchi wasn't harmed and his money was safe.

Three months later, Kaiser again helped save a life. One night, he had gone for a walk with Fiocchi's good friend John Coda, who lived above the candy store. When they reached a pier on the Hudson River, Coda threw a stick in the water and the dog jumped in to retrieve it. After

Kaiser returned with the stick, Coda somehow lost his balance and fell off the pier and into the river. Unfortunately, Coda didn't know how to swim and began thrashing in the water, screaming for help. Then he disappeared under the surface.

Seeing his companion go under, Kaiser leaped into the Hudson and swam to the spot where bubbles were coming to the surface. The dog dove under the water and, even though it was dark, managed to find the drowning man. With his teeth, Kaiser seized Coda's collar and pulled him to the surface.

The terrified man clutched the dog and nearly pulled him under, but Kaiser remained cool and helped get Coda to the pier for the dog's second heroic act of the summer.

That night, Kaiser was given an extra special treat—a steak bone. It was a small price to pay for saving another life.